ODDLY ENOUGH

PAUL JENNINGS

ODDLY ENOUGH

INTRODUCTION BY *BEACHCOMBER*

ILLUSTRATIONS BY HARO HODSON

LONDON
REINHARDT & EVANS

First Published 1950

PRINTED BY WILLIAM CLOWES & SONS LTD., LONDON AND BECCLES.

FOR MY PARENTS, BLESS THEM

ACKNOWLEDGMENTS

I am very grateful to the Editors of:

The Spectator, for permission to reprint "Ça Marche Bien", "Le Cyclisme", and part of "Report on Resistentialism"

Punch, for permission to reprint "No Atomic Trams Yet He Says", and "UB"

The *Radio Times*, for permission to reprint "Utility Concert"

Courier, for permission to reprint the review of del Huevo's play

The *Advertiser's Weekly*, for permission to reprint "The Advertising World"

Town and Country (New York) for permission to reprint "Report on Resistentialism"

and, of course, to the Editor of the *Observer* for permission to reprint everything else except "Patriot Raises Ugly Head" and "Sit Still, There". These two are *new* (advt.)

P. F. J.

INTRODUCTION

It is a pleasant surprise to-day to find a humorist who is uninfluenced by the kind of high-speed American humour which is so popular in England at the moment. There is something mechanical, something that smells of mass-production about all but the very best American humour. For myself, I quickly weary of it, and begin to wish that every joke were not a wisecrack; and that the writer would not reveal so naïvely his desperate anxiety to keep up the pace, and to force me to laugh at the point marked "laugh". This is as tiresome as facetiousness. But it is not only the American *method* which is so widely imitated. The very language of English humour is being transformed, and American slang substituted for our own slang.

The humour of Mr. Paul Jennings is English, and his method entirely his own. His effects are produced, for the most part, by discussing some preposterous statement in a deceptively reasonable manner. But while he is considering the matter quietly, and even solemnly, his imagination is kindling, and may at any moment blaze out in an outrageous absurdity. His adventures are usually in buses or trams or tubes, in streets and railway stations, and he has a voracious appetite for recondite trades, and for the odd names given to mechanical gadgets; for bye-laws, regulations, and lists of instructions. Like all people who keep their eyes wide open he is lucky in his adventures. Of all the millions who travel on the underground railways, how many would know that they advertise auctions of plant and machinery, at which the fortunate bidder may acquire centreless cutter taps, rag boilers, gang-slitting machines and fixed head routers? And who but Mr. Jennings has ever had the chance of playing a game of halma, from directions printed in German, with a man who understood German as imperfectly as himself? The halma box was discovered

> in one of those shops that sell old lithographs and Prospects, and boot-trees, and tiled pictures and 1920-ish faded yellow dresses, and old copies of the *Saturday Evening Post*, and little lead shoes, and clocks of green marble shaped like Birmingham Town Hall.

Mr. Jennings has Chesterton's habit of seeing familiar things as though he had suddenly noticed them for the first time, so that they are a surprise to him. He looks at a London tram, and observes the "Incongruous cow-catchers, suggesting that herds of steers may block the road when the tram gets into the wild country near the terminus". He is always aware of a kind of mad poetry going on all the time in the midst of modern inventions, and suspects that, though the dryads have vanished, even a bus may have its deity—"the lumbering spirits that inhabit buses". So, when he finds in Victoria Street a bronze plate on an office, marked "Activated Sludge", he lets his fancy play, instead of trying to discover what activated sludge may be.

Though Mr. Jennings' manner is usually quiet, he can enjoy letting himself go, as when he comes across a list of articles which must not be smuggled into South Africa. The list is like one of those catalogues of which Rabelais was so fond, and it includes bees, dead bodies, sashcord, sausage-casings and opium pipes. Mr. Jennings describes the scene at the Customs when an innocent-looking family is held up by the officials, and the little boy, removing his dark glasses, turns out to be "a dwarf representing a shady firm of mealie product manufacturers".

The most ambitious piece in this collection is a "Report on Resistentialism". This is a satire on the poisonous philosophies of despair, and examines in a scholarly manner the discovery of Pierre-Marie Ventre that Things are against men. *Les choses sont contre nous.* Ventre "advocates a complete withdrawal from Things", and the effect of the new philosophy on painting and music is described, and Ventre's drama "Puits Clos" is examined. A common criticism of this kind of satire is that it is facile; that the cranks of to-day need no parodist, because they unconsciously parody themselves. Mr. Jennings succeeds, I think, in producing the impression that that is exactly what is happening; that it is not he who is exaggerating their nonsense, but they who are unconsciously making fun of themselves. Nobody to-day could swear that he has not somewhere read of Dufay's new musical scale, "in which each note is seen as a point on the circumference of a circle of which the centre is the A.M.R. of each instrument. The circle must then be conceived as inside-out". If Kodak is not at work yet on a "Piece for conductors only", he may soon be. The great days of Dadaism and Surrealism were full of such pioneering work.

Mr. Jennings was fortunate enough to secure Mr. Haro Hodson, whose work is well known to readers of the *Observer*, as his illustrator. Mr. Hodson seems to me to have caught perfectly the grave expression on the faces of those who were privileged to watch the Clark-Trimble experiments with four hundred pieces of carpet.

I am happy to re-introduce the work of Mr. Jennings to those who have already enjoyed it in the *Observer*, and to introduce it to the larger public of which I am certain he is assured.   J. B. MORTON.

CONTENTS

MONEY BACK

The splendid Georgian façade and the misty sweep of
grassland down to a lake with ornamental bridge belied
the nearness of London, and gave a touch of pathos to the
occasional Londoners who passed us, smelling slightly of
damp, dark cloth. It was a wet Saturday afternoon in
March. There was distant shouting and the thud of
soggy footballs. We saw many people with dogs, many
without, many alone. Harblow was on leave from the
Army, in which he has elected to remain. We felt a little
superior to them all. We had something to talk about. We
were not merely escaping from bed-sitting rooms.

As we entered the mansion, which now serves teas, we
were talking about the Indian railway station where we

had last seen each other. I remembered the teeming families squatting round their brass drinking pots, the glistening brown bodies washing at the pumps; I remembered the curious translation of that British thing, the railway, from its proper Emett milieu of clanking Wolverhampton goods yards and Charles Keene cartoons, to the blinding, indifferent East.

Was it all over? Surely London was still a name for something in the hearts of Englishmen away from England. Surely it wasn't reduced to *this*—this neurosis of damp red brick, those horn-rimmed, close-lipped, pork-pied tabloid-readers coughing into their fag-ends in the Tube? Was the great, blind, tragic building mocking us with echoes of a vanished era of expansion and optimism; or was it here and now that the decent English, with their neat schoolchildren, were dreaming of a new order, absorbing even industrialism into a workable way of life?

The tea room was a vast cavern of a place. What would the French make of this?—a little orchestra, perhaps—certainly not utility china and a bleak serving table where one queued for single cups of tea, bread and butter, and railway cake. A notice said that the caterers solicited orders for weddings, *balls* and other functions.

A smaller card said "Special To-day, Peach Melba". Harblow, who saw nothing tragic in this, put one on his tray—a sad-looking dish filled with some opaque, orange-coloured substance with a dab of ersatz cream. We sat down in the cavern, among the children and the dogs and the murmured conversations.

Harblow gingerly took a spoonful of his Peach Melba, and then said in a confident mess anteroom voice: "This is the most hideous stuff I have ever tasted. You try it."

Rather apathetically, I did so. It certainly was awful.

I know aluminium doesn't go rusty; but if it did, that's what it would taste like. Food should be organic in origin, but this had a terrible metallic, *boring* quality—the way a penny tastes to a child licking it on an endless, boring summer afternoon. It wasn't just not nice. There was this aggressive, metallic nastiness. And yet boring. Boring food for another 20 years. I wanted to rush out to see something living, even if it was only the damp footballers.

Suddenly I realised with horror that Harblow was going to protest—*to ask for his money back*. Harblow, I thought bitterly, is the sort of man who would ask for his money back at the cinema if the projectionist, the manager and all the usherettes were shot dead by bandits two minutes before the end of the film. I sought wildly for reasons that would dissuade him, but I could think of nothing that would fend off the inevitable reply: "It's the *principle* of the thing." He strode up to the counter. . . . I felt doom all about me.

The manageress was a tired-looking woman with wispy yellow hair. She looked as though 13 hours in some enormous steamy kitchen had drained all the life out of her (no, no that was nonsense. They only made tea—and one pot at a time, at that. But maybe there was a ball to-night.) If she had been a red-faced tyrant: if she had said: "Well, you don't expect it flown from the South of France for 1s. 6d., do you?"—even if she had given Harblow a Complaint Form to fill up, it wouldn't have been so bad. But she passed the back of her hand worriedly over her forehead. She tasted it:

"Yes," she said sadly, "it's not very nice, is it? I don't know, I'm sure. We try to make something nice for people, but it's so hard to get the stuff."

I knew all about sin when she said that. We were guilty and she was innocent. I thought of her bursting excitedly into her kitchen on Friday afternoon, laden with packets of FRUTO, the Wonder Melba. "Had to queue two and a half hours," she would say, breathlessly, "but look what I've got. Let's give them Peach Melba to-morrow. The little children will love it." Far into the night she and her associates had worked, mixing the FRUTO and pouring it into hundreds of little glass dishes. Saturday morning would be passed in pleasant anticipation, waiting for the rush. *We try to make something nice.* She would go home to-night, and her husband, an engine driver on half-pay, would knock out his pipe and say, "Well, dear, how did the Peach Melba go?" She would collapse in his arms. "Oh, Jim, Jim! They asked for their money back!"

Or maybe there wasn't even a husband. . . .

I had feared a scene, people crowding round, a man in striped jersey taking her side, saying, "Ho, yus, that's right, Missus." perhaps elbowing Harblow. But this was much worse than any scene. "Yes, I suppose you'd better have your money back," she said listlessly. Harblow had the grace to look ashamed.

I wanted to rush out weeping, to buy the manageress a great big shining motor-car, to blow up London and start again with peasants. Yet so mutable and full of infinite invention are we that when I *did* go through the door I was feeling splendid, sure that the world has much to hear from England yet.

It has. Harblow, without a word, had left a half-crown under his saucer.

NO ATOMIC TRAMS YET,
HE SAYS

One of the things which will disappear in the planned world is the tram. In the new towns—I beg your pardon, community centres—there will be no place for it. The bleak yellow trams of Birmingham, the lofty-browed Edinburgh trams climbing calmly and dreamily up Leith Walk like souls in a vague dream, the strung-together trams of Belgium and Bombay, the mad forty-mile-an-hour trams of Dublin, the non-committal trams of London—these are all relics of a time when the Industrial Revolution could still produce human things like lamp-posts and the Rocket (Stephenson's).

Let us think, therefore, of the tram; of the single myopic headlight; of the two rows of eleven passengers

B

solemnly facing each other, as if some decorous parlour game were eternally about to begin; of the incongruous cow-catchers, suggesting that herds of steers may block the road when the tram gets into the wild country near the terminus.

The tram is essentially a sober vehicle. You do not find flighty cinema or perfume advertisements in trams. It is all sturdy masculine talk, of hardware, of stuffing-boxes, of trunnion-block, spigot and brass sundries factors, and of quaint Edwardian laxatives. The tram is a melancholy vehicle, perhaps reflecting the unhappiness of the wild electricity, most mysterious and dramatic of all the natural forces, at being shut up in a gawky iron wagon and compelled to run along the same dull lines every day. Most people find the tram second only to the bath for speculation. How, for instance, is a tram driven? Anybody who has watched a tram-driver knows that there is no relation at all between what he does with those two handles and what the tram does. Sometimes he turns the right-hand one clockwise and the tram stops; then he turns it a bit more clockwise, and, with sublime unreason, the tram starts again. Sometimes, when the tram is hurtling along at full speed, he suddenly whizzes both handles round with a great air of abandon (rather like that thing at parties where you do *this* with *that* hand and *that* with *this* hand), and *it makes no difference at all*. And several times I have seen a tram stop when the driver had both hands in his pockets. Especially in Edinburgh, where the driver even has a kind of shooting-stick thing to sit on.

Perhaps these men with the handles are not the real drivers at all: they are mere figureheads—possibly people who *had* to be given jobs; mad brothers of the directors, or men who knew too much, the real driving being done by a man lying underneath somewhere, like a hobo.

Most people, too, have probably wondered what would happen if a driver got in at both ends of a tram and both started to drive. They perhaps do not know that this actually happened once.

The case, although it occurred many years ago, is well known in tram circles. It appears that in a certain town there were two tram-drivers, called Stomp and Crank (there were others as well of course, but we are only concerned with these two). They were excellent drivers, but unfortunately they were fierce rivals, and when the corporation bought a new tram in 1904 they both wanted to drive it, for it had windscreens, a pretty new-fangled thing in those days. The manager couldn't get either of them to give way, so in the end they tossed for it. Stamp won. Cronk, however, could not bear this irrevocable banishment, and on the tram's maiden trip he disguised himself as the conductor and at the first stop he rushed to the other end and started to drive. The tram remained stationary, but there were ominous creakings as Tramp and Clonk recklessly increased the current. Suddenly the only passenger, Mr Ted Fooby (63), retired bender and clicker-on, who had been sitting in the middle of the tram, was amazed to find himself sprawling on the tram-lines with two half-trams speeding away in opposite directions.

Now Clamp and Tronk had been model employees for fifty years, and the manager was a kind-hearted man. In the end a compromise was worked out whereby they took it in turns each week. Even then, however, a wild urge to drive would seize Cramp while Stonk was at the controls, and vice versa. The manager still took their side, but the corporation were getting a bit fed up, what with a lawsuit from the Foobys and one thing and another, so they turned down the manager's suggestion of rubber trams, saying that they were not convinced that Tromp and Clank would relent when they saw the tram stretching. In fact they were rather afraid of the whole idea of rubber trams stretched tightly through the streets, like chewing-gum, in some Freudian nightmare. . . .

Then, of course, there is the question of who *makes* trams. One sees advertisements by the manufacturers of hurricane pipes, leadless glaze, wigs, gongs and beetle-powders· But whoever respectfully begs to inform the public that he has brought out a new tram? And how are trams delivered? Do they come in pieces, in exciting packing-cases, to be assembled actually on their lines? Or do they arrive mysteriously at night, all in one piece, and get launched by a crane among cheers and tears and fainting women?

We shall never know now.

ACTIVATED SLUDGE

It is not often one has a chance to dawdle in Victoria Street, S.W.1. For one thing, one is usually on one's way to Victoria. For another, it is always cold there, except in deep July and August. There is a curious air of a perpetual Sunday morning in an Edinburgh suburb about those gaunt black buildings. Victoria Street is a kind of geological formation, a miniature Grand Canyon with a restless, dusty sirocco of its own. One stops to look in some excellent shop window, and this evil wind, blowing sand and bits of old Government posters, drives one shiveringly on.

Most people, if they think at all about the offices in Victoria Street, probably have a confused general picture of civil engineers, the Conservative Bookshop, and a great number of Societies for This and That. If they have never dawdled—and on the non-Victoria side at that—they will never have noticed the most interesting address of all. For I am prepared to testify on oath that on the portico pillars of one building there is a bronze office sign which simply says:

ACTIVATED SLUDGE

I have not inquired too straitly into the nature of Activated Sludge. For it is an expression which has the authentic ring of a fundamental mathematical problem, the kind of classical antinomy that has always beguiled ancient philosophers, like Squaring the Circle, or Zeno's Paradoxes, or finding the Philosopher's Stone. In this concept of Activated Sludge two perfectly opposite forces are held in perfect equilibrium, like all those electrons, mesons, neutrons, protons and morons in the atom.

For consider the word "sludge". The Shorter Oxford Dictionary defines it as "thick mud". That is not quite right, but it will do. There are advertisements in American oil journals for beautiful strong machines, painted green, and called sludge pumps. One imagines the end of the hose buried in this sludge, or thick mud, drawing it up from the bowels of the earth with a horrid sucking noise, forcing it, like some lewd toothpaste, into a sludge pond, on an old part of the oilfield not wanted for anything else.

One imagines sludge as a kind of ultimate unwanted, the liquid, or at any rate viscous, equivalent of a slag heap, only capable of usefulness again after millions of years of organic change have assimilated it into the living earth once more. Sludge, one would think, is the best word in the English language to describe something inert, *unactivated.*

But there it is, with an office in Victoria Street. Activated Sludge is probably one of the countless obscure but necessary things without which our careful civilisation would fall to pieces, something which makes tremendous headlines when it is in short supply. (One remembers all that fuss about wolfram during the war.) Perhaps any municipal engineer can tell you about the great deposits of activated sludge in Merionethshire. Perhaps Britain leads the world in sludge. Perhaps even now a party of British experts is on its way to investigate an enormous vein of sludge just discovered in Rhodesia, a vein which will bring us two million pounds' worth of orders for sludge-buckets, and separators, and rotary activators.

Indeed, now that I think of it, there was a picture in my first (and last) chemistry book, called "John Dalton Collecting Marsh Gas." It showed a Constable-looking scene, with tall summery trees, and John Dalton surrounded by curious glass vessels, leaning over the bank of what appeared to be a stream. But when you looked closer you saw that it wasn't a stream at all. It was—O horrible!—a noxious black pond—a *sludge* pond, on which black bubbles, formed of some hellish gas brewed in its evil depths, were winking with heavy lechery in the slimy ooze. . . .

Perhaps, as well as evolving his theory of the atom, Dalton also discovered Activated Sludge. One can imagine the scornful laughter of the Royal Society when he read his first paper, *On The Natural Activation of Sludge;* the years of struggle; the final triumphant vindication of his views; then the great expansion period as Britain's great sludge mines were developed; the threat to our trade by the invention in 1893, by the German chemist Tumpf, of a synthetic activated sludge process; and there followed Britain's answer with the Duplex rotary activator. . . . Ah they could tell you a fine tale at Victoria-street. But it might not be so interesting.

BYE-LAWS

To writers like Baudelaire or Graham Greene, a public place in a town, with ornamental ironwork many times painted, and asphalt paths, and closely printed sheets of bye-laws, is usually the setting for some fierce cry about *ennui*, the terrible death and boredom of the city. Not for me—not when there are bye-laws to read. I am eternally fascinated both by the deathless, blithe confidence with which the writers of bye-laws start their task with the same idea as the French encyclopaedists—that of cataloguing *everything*—and by the humorous shrug of the shoulders with which they always admit, in the end, that it can't be done.

Take, for instance, this extract from the bye-laws of Grosvenor Square now trimly laid out as the setting for the Roosevelt statue:

> No unauthorised person shall exhibit, distribute, sell or offer for hire any article, commodity, pamphlet, programme *or thing* (my italics).

Observe the rise in precision from the universal "article" to the particular "programme" and the sudden switch right into transcendentals with "thing".

Bye-law prose has the endless rhythm of the tide; the crests of the waves are the summit of human confidence, forever renewed, in the *communicability* of the universe; the troughs, that puckish resignation which suddenly gets tired of the whole business. Tension and relaxation, action and contemplation, day and night—there are many allegories for it.

I now claim to have discovered the supreme masterpiece of this art-form. It is a London Transport notice which can be studied in Tottenham Court Road Tube Station (in the corner by the paying window). I have not seen it in any other station, but doubtless London Transport had more than one copy printed.

The notice is all about the articles which can be left in the cloakroom. It consists mainly of two parallel lists, neatly laid out in the well-known London Transport type. The first list says:

Charges for such articles as:

Bags	Parcels
Baskets	Portmanteaux
Boxes	Rugs
Bundles	Packmen's luggage
Cases	Sewing Machines (hand)
Coats	Sticks
Mailcarts (folding)	Typewriting machines
(folded)	Umbrellas

If removed on day of deposit or next day, 5d. For each day beyond second day, each article 2d.

Now, this in itself is fascinating enough. There is the magically alliterative opening—"Bags, baskets, boxes, bundles." There is the curious obsession with carts. There is the quaint nineteenth-century sound of two of the items—"packmen's luggage" and "typewriting machines". There is the vagueness of the expression "Charges for such articles as"—there can't be *any* article "such as" a mailcart folding (folded) *except* a mailcart, folding (folded). The wording seems to imply that the notice is just to give you an *idea*, a few suggestions about what you can leave. It is as though London Transport envisaged someone reading it and then going home and saying, "Emily, I have just seen where it says you can leave sewing machines (hand) in the cloakroom at Tottenham Court-road Tube Station. If you're not using it I think I'll take it along with my packman's luggage to-morrow."

This list, however, is pedestrian compared with the extraordinarily arbitrary, nay, surrealist selection of objects which can be left for 9d the first two days and 5d. a day thereafter:

Bass viols
Bath chairs
Bicycles (ordinary or tandem)
Cash registers
Harps
Invalid Chairs

Mailcarts (children's non-folding)
Motor-cycles (solo, uncharged)
Musical instruments on wheels
Sewing machines (treadle)
Tricycles,
Violoncellos

One scarcely knows where to begin. One of the first things one notices, perhaps, is the genius with which a microcosm of the whole physical world is suggested by a mere 12 objects, combined, on closer analysis, with such masterly handling of repetition. Thus, music is referred to no fewer than four times, "Invalid chairs" is, of course, an echo of "bath chairs". The wheel *motif* occurs *seven* times—eight if one includes the sewing machines (treadle). Note the balance between the exact specification of "mail carts (children's non-folding)" and the vague comprehensiveness of "musical instruments on wheels."

Consider again, the magical interplay of relations in the first five names. One would think that the creator of

such a juxtaposition as "cash registers" and "harps" (these are the backbone of the list and I am sure they occurred first to the compiler) would be afraid to add anything for fear of spoiling it. Not a bit of it: the pair shine like a jewel in the larger unity which enfolds them after the addition of bass viols, bath chairs, and bicycles (ordinary or tandem).

There is, alas, no room here for a full commentary on this prose poem (what, for instance, is a *charged* motor cycle?). I must pass on the marvellous coda at the end of the second list, summing up the whole notice like the *envoi* of a ballade, conveying the same fundamental bye-law thought as the word "thing" in my first example—only with how much greater artistry:

Any article of an exceptionally bulky nature, or weighing more than 112 lb.

THEIR SOUND—MY FURY

Soon after I was born
People were paying hundreds of gns.
For primitive wireless sets, which emitted various squeaky
    dins
Through an Exponential Horn
(This I should explain
To those who, like myself, in the science of Electronics
    couldn't be dopier,
Was a kind of metal cornucopia
Through which our ancestors in amazement heard The
    Nightingale and Hullo Twins and Jack Payne.)
It was so tinny
That they only listened because it was fashionable to do so
And, since it made even Caruso
Appear to *whinny*,

'They approached it in much the same way
As Dr. Johnson did the woman preacher, when he said
(I am quoting this out of my head)
"Sir, it is like a dog walking on its hind legs. One does
    not say
'It is not done well'—
One
Is too surprised to find it done
At all." (It's amazing how often he rings the bell.)
Thus, people were not so tireless
In listening to radio when it was still called wireless
Until some wretch cried "Eureka!
I have invented the Moving Coil Loudspeaker"
And, wreathed in smiles,
Proceeded to demonstrate that it was audible for *miles*.
Since then
We have been breeding a new race of men
Who, I fear,
Do not listen, but merely hear
In the bleary dawn
They totter to the radio switch with a yawn
And pass the whole day in a fourth dimension
Of news and gardening and plays and Mr. Hector Tonks,
    M.P. and the Brains Trust and In a Monastery Garden
    and other cultural items too numerous to mention.
They have their tea
While someone thunders about the habits of the English
    bee,
Never assuming,
That others might be driven nuts by this mellifluous
    booming
Their children
Must find it very bewildren

To grow up amongst people who are unable
To conduct a conversation except by shrieking across the
    table
And who think one rather a cretin
If one misses a question through listening to arguments
                          for a tax on bettin.
I am quite frank in my confession
That to return to the antique horn would be a retrogres-
    sion
And that to the youth of to-day
Earphones are as remote as the exploits of Marshal Ney
(And anyway, it *is* a bit tiring
To be anchored to the set by three feet of wiring). . . .
All I ask in this rhyme
Is: MUST it be on all the time?

THE ADVERTISING
WORLD

I shall always remember the day when Clangpan came to
be our Chief Ideas Man, Visualiser, Art Director and
Space Buyer (advertising *was* advertising in those days)
at P.B.T.F. (Pendlebury, Bostock, Tinklepenny and
Fudge. New readers begin HERE.) Old Tinklepenny had
put an advertisement in the *Advertisers Weekly:*

> "Have you ambition? Have you just pushed your boss down
> a well? Can you do multiplication up to 12's? Do you suffer
> from Depression and Moist Palms? Do you know where we
> can get any Players? If so, you may be the man we are
> looking for. The staff of this agency know about this
> advertisement."

I think old Tinklepenny was a bit surprised when the
ad. was answered by the famous Clangpan, the dynamic
stormy petrel of advertising, the paladin of publicity, the
l'enfant terrible of *l'art*, the author of. . . . . Although it
seems strange to say it now, P.B.T.F. in those days was a
very conservative agency. We only had three accounts—
Bangwhistle and Sobb Mangles (1911) Ltd., The New

C

Century Tram Corporation, and Treacle Bells, Ltd., then quite a small firm. Tinklepenny, although he wore elastic-sided boots, was a man of remarkable vision (indeed, he could often see things coming up through the floorboards, through the walls and even down the chimney that were quite invisible to the rest of us), and his main reason for creating the vacancy was, I think, his conviction that there was a great future in treacle bells. We were all so busy bringing out new schemes for new trams and mangles that no one could spare time for this account. But if Tinklepenny thought he could fob off Clangpan with Treacle Bells he was mistaken.

Clangpan's entry was typical of the man. He arrived in a pantechnicon with six carpenters and a blonde secretary. The carpenters quickly erected four of those little waist-high swing doors and installed the secretary in Tinklepenny's outer office. Then Clangpan strode in, saying as he went through each door, "Morning, J. B. Morning, T. K. Morning B. W. Morning, ff. St. J. de B. O. Hiya, Potato Crisp, will you marry me? Have all the staff come in right away."

"I have called you all here," said Clangpan, "to work out a roster for the summer hols. and to reallocate work. You, you, and you will carry on with trams and mangles. Tumpin here" (pointing at me, for that was my name) "will do Treacle Bells and Thompson's Transparent Type-writer Ribbons (used by the World's Leading Spies), an account which I have brought with me. I shall lunch with the clients and rewrite all your copy. There won't *be* any summer holidays this year—or any other year until New Century Trams are in every street and the new Leviathan Mangle is in every—er—drawing room. By the way.

what *is* a mangle? Anyone here know?'' That was typical of the man, not afraid to show ignorance, always ready to learn. One honoured him for that. It was also a lucky break for me as it happened nobody except me *did* know what a mangle was—they had merely been putting the manufacturer's specifications into good English. Briefly I explained to him the basic principle of the Leviathan, in which live coals were inserted in the hollow rollers so that the clothes were dried as well as pressed.

"Good, good, good," said Clangpan. "You others can go. I want you to stay behind, Tumpin." When we were alone except for two Caucasians in uniform who accompanied Clangpan everywhere, he went on "I am a man of

quick decisions. I see that you have the qualities of a good
Space Buyer. Think you can do it as well as Treacle
Bells? Think it over and let me know." He lit a cigarette,
Then, briskly, "Yes?" I pointed out that I had never
bought any space before, but he said kindly "It's all a
matter of drinking with the right people. Now, six space-
buyers who are friends of mine are meeting in the
Red Lion to-day. I'll tell them you're coming." He
picked up the receiver and I heard a voice say "Central Office of Information." That was typical of our
exchange.

Later in the day he asked me how I had got on. I told
him, not without pride, that I had managed to get
Clapham Common, the third floor of Claridge's and
a triangular piece of rough pasture near Cleator,
Cumberland. He beamed with pleasure. "I could tell you
had it, Tumpin," he said.

During the next few years Clangpan transformed
P.B.T.F. into the streamlined organisation it is to-day.
We were one of the first agencies to go in for market
research on a big scale. It was typical of the man that
after building up a first-class social survey system he
allowed me to have the first use of it in the now historic
Treacle Bell campaign of 1932. Up till then we had con-
tented ourselves with the slogan:

> Nobody ever falls down wells
> Who keeps a stick of Treacle Bells

illustrated by famous artists like Landseer and Phiz (or
was it Boz?)

"Now," said Clangpan, "we shall slay them with
reason." In the P.B.T.F. Treacle Bell Survey we asked a
michro—a microcc—a mikro—a sample of 45 million

people in Britain a series of carefully-chosen questions. I give the wording because it illustrated the meticulous care with which Clangpan phrased his questionnaire so as to get unbiased, objective answers:

1. You like bells, don't you?

2. You feel that you *must* have bells, in fact?

3. But ordinary bells—bells made, say, of bronze— make a hell of a row, don't they?

4. And you can't eat ordinary bells, either, can you?

5. So don't you think it would be a smashing idea to have *treacle* bells? You'd still have your bells, but they wouldn't disturb you, or anybody else, with that silly row that ordinary bells make—and think of all that treacle. *Treacle* bells. You won't forget now, will you?

The campaign based on this survey put Treacle Bells where they are to-day. We swept the country with such headlines as "6,000,000 Left-handed Women under 90 want Treacle Bells."

Ah, those were great days. Clangpan made enemies, of course. When Tinklepenny met his unfortunate death in 1933 by falling into a vat of treacle at the ceremonial opening of the Treacle Bell factory extension, Clangpan was made a director, and already there was some ill-natured talk about certain features of the accident. Pendlebury and Bostock were, of course, already dead (they had been so, in fact, since 1854). When Fudge, too, fell into a vat of treacle in 1936, some small-minded people said openly that Clangpan had pushed him in. Even the verdict of Accidental Death did not silence them. But they looked pretty silly after the *third* treacle vat death—that of Clangpan himself. I shall never forget his face as I inadvertently trod on his fingers as he clung to the edge of the vat. Advertising had lost a great figure. But, as the new Managing Director of P.B.T.F., I shall endeavour to carry on the fine work which he began.

THE LOCOMOTORIST

There is a queue reaching right outside the doors of the Motor Taxation Department. I do not wish to tax my motor—only to renew my driving licence. When I ask if I must join the queue just for that the man says "Yes" as if he were a Communist fishmonger addressing an impatient earl. All the forms are on a tiny table. Scribbling efficiently, people are crouching all round it like wasps at a jampot, so that I have to push my arm through to get a form at all.

The first one I get is for taxing "electrically-propelled carriages". The correct form is called D.L.1 (*revised December 1948*). I can't see that further driving licence forms will ever be needed, since this one appears to cover everything from "heavy locomotive" to "mowing machine or vehicle controlled by a pedestrian," so why don't they just call it D.L.? And what an extraordinary reference number it has! (9/48) (642805) Wt.42040–4226 2000m. 3/49 D.L. I simply can't imagine any filing system that would require all that. Does 2000m. mean that 2,000 *million* were printed?

Now I have to choose between filling in the form at this table, with irritating people pushing their arms through all the time and then getting in front of me in the queue, or joining the queue straight away and writing with the palm of my left hand as a desk. I decide on the latter, so that the form looks as if it had been completed by a re-tarded child. It is full of perforations where the pen has gone through.

There is something about D.L.1 which suspends rational activity and induces in me a dreamy, cosmic mood. It has the poetic quality of forcing me out of a simple, pragmatic concern with my particular problem—the renewal of my licence—into awareness of the vast social complex, of the great life that surrounds us, with its fascinating other people, walking with their mowing machines, solemnly driving their motor tricycles equipped with means for reversing, perhaps even suffering dramatic-ally from "sudden attacks of disabling giddiness or fainting"; and all most ingeniously linked together by intricate public systems and legal sanctions.

I am sure that before D.L.1 was revised (in December 1938) one merely freewheeled on the last half-dozen questions, scribbling yes, yes, yes, yes, without even read-ing them. But now they are all mixed up, so that one has to be careful. My answers were no, no, Coventry, no, yes, no, no, yes, no. "Have you studied the Highway Code?" Answer YES or NO" says Question 16 sternly: but it is a considerable anticlimax to Question 15—"Are you suffering from any disease, mental or physical, or disability which would be likely to cause the driving by you of a motor vehicle to be a source of danger to the public?"

The note to this question says that "if your estate is in the hands of the Management and Administration Department, *curator bonis* or judicial factor" you cannot even "claim to be submitted to a test." The whole thing seems unreal. If you did suffer from a mental disease and had managed to escape from the fusty, Dickensian offices of your judicial factor and join this queue, you would obviously, with a madman's cunning, answer NO and ignore the note.

Another fascinating section refers to the Groups of Vehicles. Group A, which is the only one that contains "motor car", also includes "heavy locomotive, light locomotive, motor tractor, heavy motor car . . . or motor tricycle equipped with means for reversing, but excluding any vehicle comprised in Groups B, C, D, E, or F." These Groups make a wonderful list, from trolley vehicles to those mowing machines, but it is my Group A that interests me, since it seems to imply that *I* can drive a heavy locomotive. Yes, it must be so, because a little further down it says "If you are over 17 but under 21, you may not drive a heavy locomotive . . ."—in other words, if you *are* over 21, go ahead.

What fun it would be. People eating their Sunday dinners would feel their houses trembling. The windows would begin to rattle, vases would totter and crash, as the distant rumbling grew louder. Here comes that man in his heavy locomotive, they would say. (I should be on my way to the country; for short runs about town, I should, of course, use my light locomotive.) It sounds so much better than a "heavy motor car," which I envisage as a ponderous 1914–ish vehicle with solid tyres. . . .

But this is not all. When I finally get my licence it says I can drive motor vehicles of Groups A, D and G. Group G is motor bicycles (and tricycles *not* equipped with means for reversing); and Group D is—Road Rollers. So now I shall be able to flatten out the grooves dug by my heavy locomotive.

UB

A few weeks ago there was an item of news about a man in America who was arrested for continually running into shiny new cars with his jalopy (this excellent word, pronounced to rhyme with, but not associated with "sloppy", is the American expression for an old car). When asked for an explanation he replied simply "I just don't like 'em."

How I agree with that man! I should like to take him out in UB. UB is the name of my car, which is not only a jalopy but has these fascinating letters in its registration. UB is pronounced to rhyme and is sometimes associated with "pub". It is inconceivable that my car should be called AD, or BO, or MO, let alone anything Polish or Czechoslovakian like KX or ZB. It is as much UB as a mangle is a mangle.

I bought it before the war for £7 from a clerkly sort of man who had bought it brand-new in 1928. He could hardly have gone out much in it, because he had spent every week-end doing the weekly tasks laid down in the instruction book. It was almost the same as on the day it rolled off the assembly line, when this now grey-haired man was a conveyancer, or perhaps an assayer.

On second thoughts I am pretty sure it didn't come off an assembly line at all. Cars like UB were made lovingly, one at a time, by elderly, shirt-sleeved craftsman such as one used to see in the drawings of Mr Heath Robinson— men who only twenty years previously had been building gigs, traps and phaetons. One can tell this from the position of the headlights, which are at the side of the windscreen. People who do not understand about UB ask me sarcastically where I get the acetylene these days, but that is only because they are peeved at not being able to find the battery, which is under the passenger's seat. I always see UB taking shape in a place which I visualise as a converted barn still filled with a faint smell of musty hay. Dust floats in the sunbeams filtering through a small, high window. The craftsmen are in consultation.

"Gideon," says one of them, "let us have an oil-gauge in this one."

His mate looks perturbed. "You know what we said about not buying anything outside, Eli," he says.

"Nay, Gideon, it is a thing we can make ourselves. I thought of it as I was coming through Barton's Copse this morning. Lookee here." And he goes on to explain UB's oil-gauge.

It is for this alone that I would rather have UB than my friend Harblow's car, in which the dashboard is a mass of instruments. For my oil-gauge is not an instrument at all.

It is a button. You start the engine and press this button in. If it comes out again you know the oil pressure is all right. Either it is all right or it isn't. There is none of this worrying about falling below a certain pressure (and I suspect that most people, like Harblow, don't know what this pressure is supposed to be, anyway).

It is the same with the rest of the car. Harblow would never, in his most boastful moments, say he really understands his carburettor, which has about five pipes going into it and also has an absurd frying-pan thing full of *oil* on the top, which he says lamely is an *air-cleaner*. UB has been bumbling along now for twenty years with the good old British atmosphere, which is clean enough for us. And whoever heard of cleaning air, or anything else for that matter, with *oil*? Gideon, Eli and Co. knew better. They knew that a carburettor is essentially a thing with holes in it for mixing petrol and air in a fine spray ready for explosion, and they didn't go messing about with things full of oil, which would obviously find its way eventually to these holes and block them up, in much the same way as marmalade always finds it way between one's fingers. And there is only one pipe going into my carburettor. You know where you are.

Harblow's car has the petrol tank at the back. It is connected to the engine, which is much higher up and about ten feet away, by a complicated system of pipes and taps and pumps and filters (there seems to be a mania for filtering and cleaning in modern cars). Any one of these things can go wrong, and usually does, about twelve miles from Swindon on a dark wet night. Whenever I am with him it is a thing called the automatic pump. We can't even begin to repair it until the engine has cooled down because it is right down in the bowels of the mechanism and one burns one's knuckles against the hot cylinder block. This pump seems to have about a hundred washers, which either get dropped and lost or are discovered to have been left out when the whole thing has been tightened up again. After half an hour's sucking, blowing and cursing Harblow produces a little wire gauze thing full of the most amazing geological specimens. "The filter is choked," he says indignantly, "This petrol is a scandal." Well, I buy the same petrol and it doesn't choke my filter because there isn't one. I have a theory that a strange chemical action takes place in these filters and that the petrol crystallises out. Gideon and Eli didn't have to worry about pumps, automatic or otherwise, because UB's petrol tank is behind the dashboard and the stuff just *falls* down according to the well-known laws of Isaac Newton.

Then there are the brakes. Every three months or so Harblow notices a funny smell and he gets out and finds that his rear brake linings are practically on fire. He has hydraulic brakes (*more* pipes and, I shouldn't be surprised, more filters) and to put them right it is necessary to perform a terrible operation called bleeding the master cylinder. UB's brakes, although a considerable advance in their day on the earlier models of Gideon and Eli, which probably had a stout oak block against the wheel rim operated by iron levers, are simplicity itself. They are operated by wire cables which pass over a little wheel coming down on a screw thing from the floor of the car. If the brakes are too tight you screw the wheel down a bit. It takes one minute. Bleeding the master cylinder takes Harblow three week-ends at home and then two months in a garage.

Another thing of which people like Harblow seem to be

inordinately proud is the fact that their engines are mounted on rubber. It is true that when he starts up his car during his eternal attentions to the innumerable cleaners, boosters, dust-baths, bird-bins and fly-traps the whole engine does jump about in a most insecure-looking fashion, so that you can see about ten of it. But it seems very precious to me. UB's engine is bolted firmly to the chassis, and when it is ticking over it is the mudguards of which you see about ten; there is a nice comfortable thubbing feeling as you get into the seat. Rubber is perishable, and this is one of the many reasons why you often see cars like Harblow's on scrap heaps but never cars like UB. It is because the owners have got tired of bleeding the master cylinder and adjusting the oil-filter, the petrol-filter and the air-filter and buying new blocks of rubber. You couldn't have left one of these rubber-mounted cars at the bottom of the garden throughout the whole war, as I did UB, and found it ready to drive again after fitting a new hood, new plugs, new windscreen-wiper (and, come to think of it, a new windscreen), two new tyres, new king-pins, new front spring, new cylinder head, new battery, re-wiring and re-painting, drying out the magneto in the oven, getting the dynamo re-wound and mending the leaks in the radiator.

You would have found the rubber had perished.

ÇA MARCHE BIEN

When the people of the garage in which Harblow's car seems to spend most of its time said that they couldn't provide him soon enough with a reconditioned engine or a back axle or whatever it was this time it was rather a judgment on him. We had originally planned to go to France in his car—or, rather, *in* France, since the ability to go across water is one of the few attributes he has never claimed for it—because Harblow said, "If we go in UB the French will laugh at us." It was useless to point out to him that the only cars worth having these days are those made before 1930 or after 1946, because the ones in between have the benefit neither of the divine simplicity of UB, nor of the one-year period of grace which elapses before the extraordinary and, to my mind, retrogressive complications on the modern car bring it to a standstill. Harblow's car was made in 1935, an absolutely fatal year when they were just beginning to build all those baroque bulbous-looking things round the carburettor, but he still goes round telling everyone with foolish pride what a good year it was.

So we went in UB after all. From the practically deserted quayside at Newhaven, with its silent electric cranes, their grabs disdainfully shortened to cope with UB after the S.S's and Daimlers, the boat took us slap into the middle of Dieppe on what appeared to be market-day. The majority of the passengers were French, and they were being met by an average of five relatives each. Before this vast assembly, the cars were being lifted out by the noisiest and most insecure-looking steam crane I have ever seen. I don't suppose it *was* insecure really, any more than those incredible wire railways in the Alps on which people go on not getting killed year after year. But since childhood, when I observed that the best model steam engines were the ones with horizontal boilers, I have always distrusted the ones with the boiler standing on its end. (For one thing, the fire can't heat so much of the water, can it?). The piston, which was only about a foot long, whizzed round at an enormous speed when the crane was making a wobbly turn on its axis or the thing was out of gear, but whenever it picked up a car it emitted a sort of slowing-down, groaning noise which suggested that it could only just make it.

The crane seized UB with obvious relief after a long row of shiny new cars labelled "*Export. Sportcar A.G. Zurich*," and deposited it with a flourish in the midst of the cheering spectators. The French did not exactly laugh at UB. I think they were too amazed. But they did shake

D

my faith in their famous logic. Harblow had already remarked on the extraordinary number of French cars on the roads; many of these, it is true, were modern cars with bumpers and, delightful phrase, *avertisseurs sonores*. (UB's advertiser, one of those ancient klaxons which seem to go through a couple of gears before they reach a steady note, we had left behind because age had so reduced its sonority as to make it practically inaudible.) But there were also a considerable number of what I can only call jalopies, even older than UB—strange jalopies with bodies like boats only with the sharp end at the back; old high jalopies with vertical steering columns; and we even saw one jalopy with solid tyres. I do not think the arrival of UB seriously lowered the average age of cars in France. Yet, for some reason, it was greeted on the quayside and wherever we went with cries of "*le petit tank anglais!*" except for one wonderful moment in a dark garage when a man said, "*Qu'est-ce-que c'est que vous avez là? C'est un jeep, hein?*" Almost every time we went into a garage the man would slap it casually and say "*Cinq chevaux, hein?*" and my reply "*Non, monsieur, sept-point-neuf. Presque huit,*" always produced a sensation. The economical French would make any engine with 8 *chevaux* power a car about 15 feet long (and by a quaint reversal, carry about 40 *hommes*).

It was just after Chamonix, as I now tell my 1935 friends casually, that UB suddenly and unaccountably began to boil every kilometre and shed glorious light on one of my two pieces of exotic French. I suppose everyone keeps a few outlandish words in addition to his basic vocabulary. Thus, just as I know that the German for accelerator is *Geschwindigkeitsumschaltungshebel*, I also know that the French for a swarm of bees is *un nid d'abeilles*.

When we went into a garage and explained that *l'eau bouillit toujours* the *mécanicien* (mechanic) looked at the *radiateur* (radiator) and shook his *tête* saying, "*Ah, c'est un vieux nid d'abeilles*" (an old nest of bees), 1935 motorists like Harblow have never heard of honeycomb radiators, and it took me some time to convince him that this was not just a quaint Gallic oath.

The *mécanicien* was very thorough. He replaced the lozenge in the cylinder head which we had blown out with the steam. He tested the ignition, the oil pressure, the gearbox and the brakes. He blew up the tyres, and came out for a ride with us (or with me anyway, as there wasn't room for Harblow as well) to see the water boil for himself, which it did with a fierce glub-glubbing noise before we had even got out of the town. He didn't do anything to the old nest of bees or in fact to any part of the actual water system, contenting himself with telling us that the *radiateur* was blocked up, and he gave us some *pastilles* (pastilles) which he said would *déboucher* it. We took this to mean that they would dissolve the rust and other blockages in the water.

For the next two days we amazed the inhabitants of the Jura Mountains by driving through their villages with a huge bulging red rubber bag dangling at the back of UB. It was a groundsheet filled with about two gallons of water and tied up, after stupendous efforts, with rope. Every five kilometres or so we stopped. There was no sound except the water glub-glubbing away and the tinkle-tinkle of the mountain cow-bells. We waited for the glub-glubbing to cease (the tinkle-tonkle never ceased, not even at two in the morning. I had no idea cows were so restless), and then we filled a very ornate jug, which Harblow had bought in Chamonix, from this great bladder *without undoing the rope.* It's quite easy if you don't mind it going up your sleeve. We stuffed *pastilles* into the *radiateur* until it was full of a thick brown liquid and we were afraid that any more would dissolve the *radiateur* itself. Slowly and patiently we increased our range before boiling to six, seven, ten kilometres.

Just outside Dijon we discovered what was wrong. The rubber tube from the *radiateur* to the engine (*moteur.* They would!) was absolutely solid. It had perished inside. In a rash moment I passed on to Harblow my other piece of exotic French—*caoutchouc.* As anybody in the Fourth Form will corroborate, this fantastic word actually means rubber. (Where *did* they get it from? To my mind anything, even *snerl*, or *pingleboob*, sounds more like rubber than *caoutchouc.*) When Harblow rushed into a nearby garage and informed it that "*le caoutchouc est mort dedans*" it was one of the occasions when they did laugh.

LE CYCLISME

Our first experience of *le cyclisme* is during a thunderstorm.
A motor-cyclist suddenly materialises out of the rain two
hundred yards ahead. He is coming towards us on our
side of the road. Do they, perhaps, drive on the left in
this *Département*? I think he wants us to get off the road.
I do so with a second to spare.

There follow three more motor-cyclists, all blowing
whistles but not waving, so we have evidently done what
the first one wanted. We are just outside a small village,
the single street of which is lined by a great crowd which,
by its dress, does not appear to have noticed that it is
raining. We have just time to observe that there also

seems to be a fair, with a wonderful poop-pooping steam organ, when ten cars come roaring through. Aha! we think, this is one of these famous French car-races. But as they pass we notice that each has a big yellow notice saying "*Officiel!*" There is an expectant pause, then more whistle-blowing from the other end of the village. Two gentlemen in bathing-costumes appear round the corner and pedal through in what appears to us a rather apathetic manner until we are informed that the race has a hundred laps and is not expected to finish until 11.30. It is now only ten-to-five and they have been going a mere four hours. They and the next six are received with mild enthusiasm, but suddenly a group of about twenty whirrs furiously past and the ovation is tremendous. We would like to ask whether this is because these are the men of this village or because they are leading and the people in front were really behind; but this sounds silly, even in English.

It is rather awkward getting through the village, because as soon as there is a lull in the blowing of whistles and the cries of "*Dégagez!*" the crowd spills into the road and the fair goes on, poop-pooping and all. Nobody else seems to want to go our way. In the end we have to fix it with five gendarmes all along the route, and we get a tremendous blowing of whistles and *dégagement* all to ourselves. The village shows a gratifying interest in UB.

Two days later we arrive at the town of Chamnecy, where it is obvious that they are preparing for a much bigger thing. Every other car is "*Officiel*". Banners across all the streets inform us that there is to be a *Grand Nocturne Cycliste* to-morrow. Just to bring the point home, a man drives happily round the town from dawn to dusk, one hand on the steering-wheel and the other holding a

microphone, his eyes looking upwards and sideways in
the way all holders of microphones seem to have, and
makes a non-stop appeal to his *chers amis sportifs* to turn
up in force. They do. When we join the huge throng at
the track, the same voice is adjuring its dear sportive
friends not to press themselves upon the fence and spill

themselves upon the *piste*, because this not only annoys the
racers but also destroys the very costly material purchased
for us all by the *Comité des Fêtes*.

The main contest is between some people called *Les
As de France* and a collection of local talent, among which
is one Bobillard, who, the loud-speaker informs us during
the *présentation des coureurs*, is the *champion de vitesse du monde*.
But, as the *présentation*, in which names are called out one
by one and the gentlemen in bathing-costumes wheel
their bicycles up to the starting-line, gets into its stride, it

seems that nearly everyone is a champion of *something*. The first race is called the *éliminatoire*, in which the last man in each lap retires. We can understand this, as there are about two hundred *coureurs*. Also the system of placing seems reasonable enough. But we do not understand the note in the programme about the next two races, the *individuelles*. This reads:

> "Dans les deux épreuves individuelles, à chaque sprint, il est attribué aux 4 premiers coureurs classés, 4, 3, 2 et 1 point. Au dernier sprint, les points sont doublés. Toutefois, le ou les coureurs terminant la course avec au moins 50 secondes d'avance seront classés en tête, les points n'intervenant que pour départager les coureurs à l'égalité de temps."

This gives us that awful feeling one used to have in exams, when one knew what every word meant, but they simply didn't add up to anything. How *can* the points only intervene to share out the runners at the equality of time? And whatever does "the where the runners ending at least 50 seconds ahead will be classed ahead" mean? Is it, perhaps, a misprint?

And how does one *know* when there is a sprint, anyway? But this question at least is answered for us as soon as the race begins. "*Chers amis sportifs*," says the loud-speaker, "*tes sprins seront annoncés sur le hautparleur*". And announced they are, apparently whenever the announcer feels like it. Or perhaps it is whenever anyone feels like offering a prize on the spur of the moment, for after a few laps, when Bobillard and others have begun to draw away from the main body, the loud-speaker begins to make announcements like this: "*Mme Dupont, de la pâtisserie de l'Avenue Carnot, vient d'offrir un prix généreux de cinq cent francs pour le premier coureur de platon dans ce sprint*". We gather from a bystander that the platoon is the main body of contestants who are soon so far behind Bobillard and the Aces of France that they are in front of them (so perhaps we were right, back in the village, after all). Eventually they are all together again. Then Bobillard and Co. forge ahead once more, taking a few more of the platoon with them until it is difficult to see which *is* the platoon and exactly who is winning. But the announcer apparently has his finger on things, because every now and then he informs us that So-and-so is *deux tours en avance* and one of his sportive friends is always offering another prize, sometimes for the best time in the next sprint by *anybody*, but more often just for the platoon, which by now is practically indistinguishable. There are prizes for everyone in this race. We begin to see what all those *officiels* are for. There must be one to watch the progress and record the winnings of each man.

But we still do not understand this business of the equality of time. It is rather difficult to ask any of the spectators, as they are all busily either writing down points or shouting. Harblow gives it up after pointing to the words *50 secondes en avance* and saying "*en avance de quoi, Monsieur?*" and being met with a torrent of French of which the only word he can catch is "*éliminatoire*". We are sure we have had that one already. We leave as the last race, called *Petit Tour de France*, is beginning. We go to see a very long film. When we come out the cyclists are swishing past under the bright lights. But we go back to UB. It seems to us a much better way to do a tour of France. We are a long way from Chamnecy when I suddenly realise that *le ou les* doesn't mean "the where the" but "the *or* the". I don't think Harblow has got it even yet.

THE ROOT OF EVIL

Before the war

You could be fairly certain that, whatever you found in tins, it wouldn't be a bore;

You didn't need an expert in plannery

To tell you that only exotic things, like apricots or anchovies, justified the expense of a cannery,

Things which, if they weren't in tins, the problem of having them at all would be much thornier—

Such as pineapples, and those little orangey things, and Yellow Cling Peaches in Syrup, from California.

So I view with alarm

The present tendency to tin foods devoid of all charm,

Foods which depress you, like the books of Schopenhauer,

And are not worth your trouble with the tin and the openhauer;

Rhubarb, like sour green lamp wick; and carrots, and many another doleful vegetable

Which you could buy from barrows, or grow yourself, or which from the market is quite fetchitable.

You don't need the wisdom of Plato

To wonder if it isn't a waste of tin, to tin a thing like a potato.

The contents of tins get prosier and prosier

Until, dreariest of all this utility ambrosia,

At the end of a dreary (for "dreary" is a word I am forced to repeat) route,

We come to tinned *beetroot*,

No one with taste will be my inomy

When I say beetroot is a philosophical contradiction, or antinomy;

It is so insipid you would swear it isn't there at all, yet it
    has what Descartes calls extension;
Beetroot is boredom with a third dimension.
Beetroot is at the bottom end of creation. At the top end,
    to make my point clearer,
You have small, intense, very-much-existing things, like
    diamonds or Miss Moira Shearer;
At the other end there is beetroot—soggy, brackish,
    oozing, occupying a lot of spaos,
And about as attractive as Primeval Chaos;
Indeed, my vision of Chaos, before the Creation
Is a sodden, heaving, dull, bloodshot mass of beetroot
    without form of limitation:
Then came man. Among his achievements are Chartres
    and the Bach B Minor, and among his sins
Is beetroot in tins.

FAREWELL TO GAS COYS

On May 1, while baroque façades threw back the echoes of comradely feet in Europe's capitals, while school-mistresses on draughty village greens helplessly watched the class half-wit turn the wrong way with her maypole ribbon, reducing the whole dance to a cumulative, night-mare tangle, while Spring kissed the face of the West—on that day the North Thames Gas Board was created.

I have just been reading a notice in one of those gas showrooms where everything works by gas except the telephone (and I daresay they're experimenting with *that*). It says:

"The 1st of May, 1949, is the starting date of the new North Thames Gas Board in which are vested the 12 gas undertakings shown in this map:

1. Uxbridge, Maidenhead and District Gas Coy.
2. Slough Gas Coy.
3. Windsor Royal Gas Coy.
4. The Ascot District Gas Coy.
5. The Chertsey Gas Consumers' Coy.
6. The Gas Light and Coke Coy.
7. The North Middlesex Gas Coy.
8. Hornsey Gas Coy.
9. Commercial Gas Coy.
10. Lea Bridge District Gas Coy.
11. Romford Gas Coy.
12. Shoeburyness."

I wish the North Thames Gas Board nothing if not success. But what a sterile sound there is about this title! It seems a pretty poor substitute for the exuberant gas-age multiplicity of all those splendid gas coys which it replaces.

Consider, for instance, the pleasant, rural sound of the Uxbridge, Maidenhead, Wycombe and District Gas Coy. One sees the gasman, in 1871, with "U.M.W. and D. Gas Coy." in gold letters on his cap, wearing a beard and sidewhiskers down to *here*, coming to read the meters in some little Maidenhead back street, ending by the river in a cul-de-sac: he is a familiar sight to the girls in pinafores and the boys in knickerbockers playing hop-scotch. I am sure that this coy, as well as the Ascot District Gas Coy. and, of course, the Windsor Royal Gas Coy, have the nice old-fashioned gasometers painted green with an external framework of white girders, and never higher than they are broad. The gasworks themselves have ivy growing round them. They are long, low dark buildings because they have the old horizontal retorts. Their gas goes to polished geysers in quiet bathrooms where nothing has been changed, except the blue plastic curtains, for the last 60 years. (That was when these spare bedrooms were converted.) Stay, there has been one change—the electric light, its conduit pipes bulging under the wall paper. This was done in 1921.

Slough Gas Coy, however, as befits the humming industry of this curious suburban Magnitogorsk, is very modern. I am sure the Slough Gas Coy has vertical retorts. I am sure, too, that it has a research laboratory, where chemists produce all those remarkable nylons and gramophone records and, for all I know, boiled sweets and mushroom pie, which they say are by-products of coaltar, but which never seem to appear in the shops. (Maybe these are academic successes. Maybe it takes a million gallons of tar to make just one pair of nylons, which the chemist then gives to his wife.)

The Chertsey Gas Consumers' Coy, on the other hand, was obviously an interesting social experiment. Back in the days when retired people were beginning to build their houses on the bosky banks of Chertsey they were very happy in the summer, but during the long winter evenings they found oil lamps irksome after the gaslit city. Neighbouring gas coys, approached for a supply, rubbed their hands gleefully, thinking: "Ah, we're on a good thing here. All retired people with plenty of money. And we can charge them for extra pipeage." But the Chertsey people, outraged, held a meeting in the school hall. Led by a kind of middle-class Robert Owen, they resolved to form their own coy—a *consumers'* coy. For the first five years they made the gas themselves in a pleasant little Gothic gasworks, surrounded by willows, in a bend of the river (of course they hired navvies to lay the pipes and do the rough work). Later the coy was taken over by professional gas-makers, but the consumers have always retained the controlling interest.

With the other gas coys, particularly the Gas Light and Coke, we are already leaving these splendid individualists for the modern age of amalgamation. The Commercial Gas Coy.—I'm sure they make splendid gas, but you can probably only buy it in quantity, if you have a foundry or a die-stamping works, or a laundry

The terse expression "Shoeburyness" suggests that there is some great institution there needing no further introduction to gas people. Just as Oxford men speak of "Univ." as wartime officers spoke of "Wrotham", so gas men say colloquially to one another "I'm going on a course as Shoe." Yes, that's it; a gas college, with a model gas works and a fine playing field, separated by a line of poplars and a white wooden fence from the wide salty estuary.

Ah, Shoeburyness! Ah, Hornsey, Lea Bridge, Romford! These were flying voices heard on the wind. Now they are swallowed up for ever in the grey anonymity of the North Thames Gas Board, and what makes it sadder is the suspicion that the gas coys themselves don't seem to mind much either way. I have seen no men with banners saying, in that silly banner style halfway between a headline and a short story, "North Thames Gas Board Unfair to Hornsey!" Nor, on the other hand, were there speeches and fireworks and three-legged races and still lemonade and openings with silver keys on May 1. In fact, a tremendous number of gas people simply took a day off and stayed apathetically at home. For May 1 was a Sunday.

PSYCHOLOGICAL GRADING

All British sociologists will welcome the Report of the
Royal Commission for Psychological Grading in Busy
Places, published this week for the Ministry of Development and Printing, for it represents the first real official
attempt to cope with the problem in modern society of
complication-neurosis.

This is a condition which can best be explained to the
laymen by actual examples. Let us imagine a suburban
branch Post Office with, say, six positions—Stamps,
Savings, Money Orders, Position Closed, Pensions and
Allowances, and Telegrams. An ordinary customer (in
the sociologists' jargon, a neutral counter unit, or N.C.U.)
such as the reader or the writer of this article—a person,

therefore, entirely free from complication-neurosis—goes in to buy a book of stamps. He is preceded in the queue by a complication-neurotic who, perhaps, wishes to send a parcel to the Virgin Isles, a possession of the U.S.A. The clerk looks dubious, then calls someone from an inner office with a glass door. They fetch down a big book—the Post Office Guide. They find the section on the Virgin Isles.

"Ah," murmurs the First Clerk, "Customs Declaration 'A' ".

They are not quite sure what this is, so they flip rather aimlessly through the pages until it occurs to Clerk Two to look up "Customs" in the Index. They find it and Clerk One reads, in an unsure sort of voice, "Two kinds of customs declaration form are in use, namely an adhesive form to be affixed to the parcel (mainly for Empire use), and a non-adhesive form (for most foreign countries). Two or more copies of the latter form may be required, see pp. 110–209."

But pp. 110–209 are merely the alphabetical section covering the world's countries, containing the bit about the Virgin Isles where Clerk One started. We are in a vicious circle. But this is only the beginning. When they have finally decided about the Customs, Clerk Two says, "What's in the parcel?"

"Well, it's a kind of model I made," says the woman helplessly, "and a few potatoes."

"Potatoes, eh?" says Clerk One doubtfully. More page-flicking, then, "I'm afraid we can't accept it, ma'am." For under "Prohibited Articles" it says, for the Virgin Isles:

"*Letters, cotton seed, cotton and cotton seed products (except oil, manufactured cotton and cotton waste; see below); feathers and*

E

skins of wild birds (except ostrich feathers) unless for educational purposes; films or pictorial representations of prize fights; intoxicating liquors; potatoes. . . ."

And so on, while all the normal person or N.C.U. wants is this book of stamps. Not only Post Offices are affected by the spread of complication-neurosis. Evidence submitted to the Commission shows that most of the people who want a simple third-class return to Birmingham in a hurry are preceded by the sort of man who wants to go to an obscure place in the Hebrides. He has voluminous inquiries about sailing tickets and ration books and *insurance*. His ticket, instead of being issued quickly with a metallic thump from a machine, has to be laboriously written out on a duplicate form with long footnotes about "Messrs. MacBrayne's Services." In a bank, an N.C.U. who merely wishes to cash a cheque for £5 will be preceded by someone with a battered attaché case full of little blue bags full of pennies and complicated company accounts.

The Commission's Report recommends a revolutionary technique of psychological grading, to be tried out experimentally at first in Post Offices.

"We are in entire agreement with the experts who have given evidence," it says, "that the present division of Post Offices into operational functions is arbitrary and inefficient. We therefore recommend a form of Psychological Grading. In a Six-Position Post Office two of the positions should be labelled 'SIMPLE'. The remaining four should be labelled 'COMPLICATED'. Counter units should be met at the door of the Post Office by a trained psychologist who by the answer given to some such question as 'Good morning sir (or madam); what do you require?' would be able to deduce the degree, if any, of complication-neurosis, and direct the counter-unit accordingly."

I need hardly point out the effect on our social life if the Report is acted upon. Normal people like the reader, or the writer, of this article will be able to pop quickly in and out of the Post Office, even at the busiest times. Complication-neurotics will have a special part of the Post Office all to themselves, screened off with trellis and artificial roses; there will be little tables where they can discuss their problems with fellow-spirits all day long over a cup of Post Office coffee.

The re-alignment of staff will mean an overall increase in Functionary Time (F.T.) without the corresponding increase in Functionary Units which sociologists previously thought this must involve. The Report, recognising the existing shortage of psychologists, outlines a scheme for

Regional Training Colleges giving a special one-year course. In the Report's concluding words, "the initial expense should soon be repaid, since from Post Offices it is a short step to railway booking offices, banks and shops, and we may therefore look forward confidently to an efficient rationalisation of the whole of our public life."

TRAMOPHILIA

It must baffle tram enthusiasts, the way the public go on assuming without much serious thought at all that buses are more progressive.

There are thousands of tram enthusiasts. On the editorial page of their magazine, the *Modern Tramway*, it says they are affiliated to "the N.V.B.S. (Holland); the Association Belge des Amis de Chemins de Fer (Belgium); the Electric Railroaders' Association (U.S.A.); the Association Française des Amis des Chemins de Fer

(France); Australasian Railway and Locomotive Society, the Central Electric Railroaders' Association and the Town and Country Planning Association and Stichting Tram-Archief (Holland)''. And in *50 Questions and Answers about Trams* it says that ''the Light Railway Transport League was founded by a number of men and women in all walks of life who felt that the tram was not receiving a fair deal''.

Their literature is full of every conceivable argument in favour of trams, not forgetting the help given by tramlines to fog-stranded motorists, and even the advantages of a tram system in air raids; for, says Answer No. 37 gravely, ''A heavy bomb would usually . . . cause severe damage to pipes and cables, all of which had to be repaired with weeks of labour before the surface could be replaced. On the other hand, it was the work of a few hours only to lay a length or two of new rail bridging over the crater, supported temporarily from below, and restore tram services at once. As a result it became a common sight, during the 'Blitz' to see road signs TRAMS ONLY.''

They point out, disconcertingly, that the rates always go up wherever there is a switch over to buses. Of course old-fashioned trams look silly, they say crossly; so do old-fashioned buses; but just you turn to page 23 and see our artist's conception of the trams of the future . . . and all the public does is to shift from one foot to the other, and grin uneasily, and go right on buying more buses. They give what Cardinal Newman calls a notional assent, not a real one, to the economic superiority of trams.

Perhaps the explanation lies in a fact which has been overlooked by all tram psychologists hitherto—the extraordinary similarity of a tram to a greenhouse. The trouble with trams is that they don't look like things intended to move at all. They look, as I say, like greenhouses—and double-fronted greenhouses at that. An old tram is an old greenhouse, and a streamlined tram is simply a streamlined greenhouse, and what the public is saying to itself in its subconscious is, "Good heavens, it *moves!*" Whenever the wheels come to a join in the rails, they go over it with a deadweight, heavy, unspeedy sound, like a piano being wheeled over a tiled kitchen floor. Indeed, when you consider the mountainous height of a tram, its wheels do seem as insignificant as castors. A tram is the perfect, and probably only, justification for that phrase with which the writers of insurance policies and bye-laws love to describe everything from a lift to an express train—a "moving platform".

And what *makes* it move? It seems incredible to me, as I sit in the green, glassy space, feeling as if I were in a small Crystal Palace (or a greenhouse, in fact), that there should be powerful groaning motors, and gongs, and cowcatchers, and brakeshoes, and all the statutory apparatus of public motion underneath that platform which is already so near the ground. The public likes, in some obscure way, to be *associated* with its motion. There is, no doubt, for instance, about the function of a bus. How this handrail throbs; what a nice, businesslike, enginey smell; look, there is the driver doing things we all understand—changing gear, pulling on the handbrake. It is very different from those meaningless handle-twirlings which seem to stop or start a tram without any visible logic. The bus possesses the enormous advantage of familiarity. If trams are all that good, we feel, why isn't the tram-pattern repeated in our individual lives as the bus-pattern is repeated in cars? Why aren't there showrooms full of family trams, and even little two-seater sports trams, eh? Where do we get this sad feeling that trams are going the way of dinosaurs?

These subconscious doubts of the public are prompted by that very spaciousness which the tram enthusiasts think is such an advantage (To seat 70 Persons, they say proudly). They will not be got over, therefore, by mere streamlining; and in any case so many tramlines go through narrow streets where it always seems to be Saturday afternoon, with thousands of people shuffling past shop windows full of chromium kettles and radios and rather dreary-looking pink underwear. It is no good having trams designed for an autobahn, or at least for Blackpool Promenade, in these surroundings.

Yet, as the tram enthusiasts point out, it would be criminal to scrap the rails and poles, and of course, the trams, now that we have them. It seems to me the obvious

solution lies in a compromise. Why not give up *fighting* this greenhouse idea? Why not accept it? We already have mobile canteens, and in a turning off Oxford Street there is even a mobile dental clinic, so why not mobile greenhouses? Think of it—the duckboard floor (there already in many trams), the drowsy, damp, ferny smell, the tropical heat, the great purple and orange blossoms, the little wooden tabs pointed at one end saying *Lycopodium clavatum* and *selaginella*—and all the time one could be rumbling solemnly along the street. Perhaps there could be specialisation, with tomato trams and palm trams. When enough trams had been converted to satisfy the demand for mobile greenhouses, the remainder could be stationed in loop lines strategically all over the city. Let buses go out to the green belt. The trams could provide one in themselves.

PUNCTURE

If there are any critics in the next century, the impersonal age of Aldous Huxley and Orwell, it is possible that they will talk about motor cars as we now talk about cathedrals. Just as experts to-day say that the plain spire at Chartres is "pure" and the ornate one is "decadent" so these motor critics will speak of the "great" period of the twenties.

My car, a 1928 Austin Seven whose number plate bears the apt monosyllable UB, belongs to this period. It is a "pure" car. Decadence begins when function is overlaid and concealed, when the car ceases to be a system of steel and rubber for getting from A to B and tries to become something else—a flatlet, or a small cocktail bar, with carpets and radio. In UB one never forgets that one is in a *car*. Large pieces of the classically simple engine project companionably through the floorboards. The oil gauge is a button which comes out on the dashboard (the *dashboard* not the baroque "instrument panel"). You press this button in, and if it comes out again the oil is all right; in fact the oil is so all right that it squeezes past the button and drips slowly down on to my trousers unless I periodically wipe it away.

I can thus never become dangerously absent-minded on the road; I am always reminded that I am in a *machine*. But it is a machine perfectly capable of taking me all round France, where the *garagistes* would drop work on the shiny limousines of Belgians and crowd round, saying: "*Ah, c'est un Rosingarde*." I used to think this was a poetic allusion to the steed of some legendary hero until I found that the Rosingarde is a French make of car, now defunct. I am admitted to the brotherhood of garages everywhere.

In England this is generally over punctures, for the tyres are UB's weakest point. They are thin, motor-cyclish things that grip the wheel with a kind of nervous tension, and can only be removed or fitted with violent yet controlled effort. When I have a puncture it is much more difficult than on a 10-ton lorry.

The trouble is that it always happens on a Sunday, when in all garages, there is only one man, and he is too busy with the petrol pumps to do anything for me. The last time it happened on one of the hottest Sundays of the year, I started work in a great lonely garage, at half past two. The puncture was mended easily enough and then, as usual, I couldn't get the cover back. I got mad with it and tried to bang it on with an iron pipe. Cars full of cool-looking people kept coming in for petrol. They would look at the litter of equipment, at UB so skeleton-like and static on the jack, at me with this pipe. . . .

When other people do this job they seem to be able to get two-thirds of the cover on straight away. Then they jump solemnly on it, smoking their pipes and making light conversation, as they work their way round the remaining third. But as fast as I do this the thing slips off at the other end and I simply chase it all round the wheel. Once I hit the cover on the edge and the wheel jumped up and banged me on the knee.

At last it was on. I trundled the wheel over to the compressed air thing to inflate it. I held the nozzle to the valve for some time, then gave the tyre a complacent squeeze to see if it was hard enough. It was absolutely flat. A great hole had been squeezed in the inner tube.

I dismantled the whole thing and mended this second, far more serious puncture with a patch as big as the sole of a shoe. Then I found I couldn't test it in water, because the garage man had gone away for his tea and locked up the workshop part where the tap was. However, the garage was near the Thames. I threaded my way through the picnic parties, feeling rather like Phaethon when he crashed from the sun-chariot; why couldn't I have come by Green Line, like all these honest people, instead of having delusions of grandeur about being a motorist? I tried to look as if I was testing the tube for someone's small girl.

I was still trying to get that cover on again when the garage man came with a cup of tea. I reproached myself for having bracketed him with all the people in shiny black saloons. He turned the starting handle and said, "Ah, good compression you've got there. They're marvellous things." Then he helped me with the tyre, performing a grave stamping dance on the wheel. When he came to the tight bit he simply fetched out a great lead mallet and delivered three terrible blows, and it was on. He wasn't even out of breath. "Tyres are the only snag on these," he said. He was brotherly, not superior. He accepted me as one who could have done it equally well if I had happened to possess a lead mallet.

We reassembled UB. I raced the engine, a pure motorist once more. With my foot on the clutch, I asked him how much.

"That's all right," he said. "I've got one of these myself."

LET THERE BE RAILINGS

This is not a joyful poem. In fact it is a lament, full of sad
    cadences and plangent wailings
For railings.
Let others sigh for cream and steak and such obvious
    amenities of city and subbub,
I go to the root. . . . Railings, these are the subject of my
    protest, my hubbub;

Railings, formally dividing land into *tuus* and *meus*,
Symbol of orderly, confident days, when 6d bought 20
    Pleus:
Railings, with their curious unsharp spikes,
As civilised and restrained as the truncheon, not really
    hurting anyone, even burglars or agitators in riots
    and strikes:
Edwardian railings, with suffragettes clamped on;
Wrought, or cast in foundries, at Smethwick or Wolver-
    hampton.

No one wreaks railings now, no lads are apprenticed
To replace the stumps left on those little low walls as if by
    some bungling dentist.
I do not believe the official story
That railings were melted down for glory.

I do not believe that any campaign, French, Italian,
    Rhine or Tunisian,
Was helped in the slightest by railing-Spitfires, or railing-
    tanks, or even railing-ammunition.
You've only got to look at the raw materials of railings, to
    see at once that these are low-grade metals,
Useless for anything more warlike than military saucepans,
    or kettles.
No, this was one of our wartime mistakes. . . .
There is probably a vast railing dump still, in the Mid-
    lands, or up in the Lakes,
Where the Ordnance Corps, encamped under the trees,
Say daily, "What shall we do with these?".

    Come, Powers That Be, turn not your face:
    Restore the Town its antique grace,
    Cast not our Railings in the fire
    Lest all rise up in dreadful ire
    And, every ordinance forgetting—

conduct a massacre of these people, whoever they are, that
have decided to replace our splendid railings with un-
speakably cheap, vulgar, utility, chicken-run WIRE
NETTING.

HOW TO SPIEL HALMA

The other day, when I was in one of those shops that sell old lithographs and Prospects, and boot-trees, and tiled pictures, and 1920–ish faded yellow dresses, and old copies of the *Saturday Evening Post*, and little lead shoes, and clocks of green marble shaped like Birmingham Town Hall, I found a dusty old box containing a game of Halma. In German.

I bought it, because the instructions looked so fascinating. I am not what you would call fluent in German. I knew just enough for me to bumble along in a half-understanding daze, feeling comfortably that by knowing just a few more words I could speak it like a native. I desist from actually learning these few more words because I know that in fact this would be a dreary process extending over several years while I found out about things like *schicksal* and *empfindsamkeit;* and because I also know that during the first half of this period the pleasant sense of comprehension which I feel now would diminish rather than increase.

My friend Harblow doesn't really know any more German than I do. But he is never content to allow a German sentence to remain merely a matter for pleasant speculation. As soon as he discovered my Halma, nothing would please him but that we should evolve a theory of the game from the extremely explicit-looking set of instructions on the lid of the box, and actually play.

Neither of us had played Halma before, but Harblow pointed out that the board seemed straightforward enough, like a chess-board seen through a telescope the wrong way round, and with zigzag enclosures in each corner. "Now, let's try the first paragraph," said Harblow briskly, and he read on:

> *An diesem Spiel können sich 2 bis 4 Personen beteiligen, von denen jede eine Farbe wählt, und damit, wenn 2 Personen spielen, einen grofsen Hof mit 19 Steinen, wenn 4 Personen spielen einen kleinen Hof mit 13 Steinen besetzt.*

The only difficult words here seemed to be *beteiligen* and *wählt* (I just happened to know that *Farbe* is "colour"). Our (mainly my) translation ran thus: "At this Game 2 or 4 Persons can betake themselves and each of these wears a Colour and damn it, when 2 Persons play, a big House with 19 Stones, when 4 Persons play, he besets a little House with 13 stones."

It was clear enough for me. It conjured up a pleasant picture of these Persons wearing their Colours and heraldically besetting each other's Houses like something in a Book of Hours. "Damn it" I took to be an idiomatic way of saying that the real way to play this Game is with

4 Persons. Of course, if you must, you can play with 2 Persons, but damn it, it's a pretty poor show. Harblow, however, insisted that *damit* means "with that" or "therewith," so I allowed this, to pacify him; although it didn't seem to make any more sense.

The next sentence said: "The Players now try so quickly as possible with their Stones to beset the House of the Against-man (*Gegner*) and he is the self-same Winner (*Gewinner*) who the first *gelingt*." Even Harblow had no theory for *gelingt*, so we went on to the main paragraph, a magnificent jumble of instructions of which we could not translate any particular sentence except one; but the general sense was that you got to the Against-man's House by the process of *überspringen* or overspringing, as in draughts. The sentence we did understand was *Es kann auf diese Weise eine ganze Reihe von Steinen übersprungen werden*—in this way it can a whole Row of Stones be oversprung.

We started to play, with 19 Stones (damn it), and we moved one at a time to beset each other's Houses until our forces met in the *Mittel* (Middle) of the *Feld* (Field). Suddenly Harblow, by a most curious progression involving horizontal, vertical *and* diagonal moves, oversprang five of my stones and arrived behind my zigzag thing. To my protests at the obvious irregularity of this he replied: "Well, it says here that you can move *auch seitwärts oder rückwärts*," as if that settled it.

"Well, what does that mean?" I said.

"Either sideways or—well, *rückwärts*. I am sure 'forwards' is *vorwärts*, and you couldn't want to move backwards, so *rückwärts* must be one of these untranslatable words for the silly way a knight moves in chess."

"What way is that?"

"Er—two forwards and one sideways."

"I'm sure it's two sideways and one forwards." (We don't know much about chess either.)

In the end we agreed that you could overspring a Stone that was next to you in *any* direction. When I jumped over some of my own as well as Harblow's Stones to beset his House he objected, but I pointed out to him that it was possible *über eigene und fremde Steine fortzuspringen*—over own and strange Stones to jump strongly. I had him there.

As the game progressed, if you can call it that, it began to dawn on us that we were not clear what was meant exactly by *besetting*. At the beginning we had agreed that when you oversprang the Against-man's Stone you did not remove it from the board, as in draughts, because if you did this neither *Spieler* would have any Stones left to beset the Against-man's House *with*. On the other hand, if there were not some system of being sent back to base how could this sentence be construed?:

der Gegner muss natürlich wiederum danach trachten, diesen Stein womöglich in dem eigenen Hof des Spielers einzuschliessen.

The obvious meaning of this was that the Against-man must naturally again after that treat, this Stone how possibly in the own House of the Player to shut in. It obviously implied arriving before the Against-man's House with pretty large forces, a thing quite impossible to achieve by either party, however cunning, if being oversprung meant the loss of a Stone every time. And another thing that rather militated against anybody shutting anybody else in was the fact that it was perfectly easy for both *Spielers* to evacuate their Houses completely, long before the Against-man arrived anywhere near the scene.

So the game rather petered out. Harblow's view, for

which he can offer no proof, is that the rules we evolved
would work all right with 4 Persons. But, of course, the
difficulty is to find 2 other Persons whose knowledge of
German is exactly the same as our own.

THE 113 BUS

It was the doldrum hour of 9 o'clock on Saturday night, and my only companions in the bus were two or three anonymous-looking women and a self-contained family in the front seat—parents with a small girl who kept counting up to thirty. We were going up Hendon Way— an oddly heroic-sounding name for this arterial road, lined with semi-detached houses, which drives a wedge of domestic green into the Victorian railways and panel-beating works of North London. It was, as usual, a crawler bus, determined not to pass the one in front. It stopped, to pick up a passenger, with a careful, even deceleration like a man with lumbago lowering himself into a chair, and moved off in the same way.

The newcomer looked about 55. He had smooth, soft white hair, a long, firm mouth, a lined cerebral face with black horn-rimmed glasses. He looked like a senior clerk in a law office.

But he wasn't. "Does this bus go to Piccadilly?" he asked. It was not exactly an American voice. It was the voice, perhaps, of an Englishman who had long lived in America; or perhaps a Canadian ship's engineer, a cosmopolitan whose only home for thirty years had been hotels in Bombay and Sydney and Buenos Aires. He certainly didn't belong to bourgeois Hendon Way.

The conductor's reply was simple and quite courteously "No." He was a boy with a round, ruddy rather dreamy face and damp, fair hair—an East Anglian type. He looked like a good swimmer.

There followed this conversation, all in normal conversational tones:

"Well, where does it go?"

"Edgware."

"Oh, some feller told me it goes to Piccadilly." (It does, the other way.)

"No. We go to Edgware."

"Well, does it go to Charing Cross?"

"No" (dispassionately) " —— Edgware."

"Is there anything at Edgware? I wanna go to a night-club or somethin'. Can I get to *Oxford Circus* from Edgware?" For years he had carried these fabulous names in his heart and all he had seen so far was Hendon Way.

"Yes, I expect you could get a train."

"Ah, well, I guess I'll go to Edgware. How much is it?"

"Eightpence."

I couldn't believe my ears. We were only about three miles from Piccadilly. I sat in a trance as the ticket, the *eightpenny* ticket, was punched and sold. I had the impression that I was the only one who had even heard this extraordinary dialogue. Normally a voice has only to be slightly unusual, emphatic, over-cultured, alcoholic, and the whole bus listens entranced. But the family remained absorbed in itself, the women stared primly into nothing. Was I the only one interested in the fate of this lonely pleasure-seeker?

I thought of this man, getting out of the bus at the turning-round place in Edgware. It would be a desolate, clinker-surfaced piece of waste land, bordered by a few trees rustling in the cold September wind. Behind, the suburban Hertfordshire hills stretching into the gloomy night. There would be a mobile canteen for the busmen. Edgware people would be coming out of a small cinema. What would they say when he asked for the night-club area? How would he compare this with those nights out with the boys so many years ago, in Marseilles and Montreal? I thought of the outrageous train journey—Edgware to Charing Cross—so casually recommended.

Suddenly the power of action returned. I turned round and explained that he had only to get on a 113 going the other way and he would be in Piccadilly in half an hour. "Ah, yes, you could do that," agreed the conductor equably. The traveller thanked me and got out.

The conductor gave me a smile which said plainly, "That was an odd fellow, wasn't it?"

I found myself talking. "I couldn't let him go all the way to Edgware," I said, apologetically.

"Ah well," said the conductor, "I thought I might as well let him go. *He'd bought his ticket*."

My italics.

BRITISH RAILWAYS

There is something curiously unsatisfactory and pedestrian about the title "British Railways". It is a matter of geography, not of politics or economics, that there are *four* railway systems in Britain, and no amount of unification, in name or even in rolling stock, will alter this. Nobody quite believes in the title "British Railways" because the old names were so much more poetically apposite. LNER, pronounced as a word, has a thin sneering, east-wind sound, suggestive of those long, cold stretches by the North Sea. GWR is the sort of noise made by a large, round-eyed but essentially domesticated dog, worrying playfully through Mendip tunnels.

The GWR plays at being industrial, but everybody

knows that Paddington really leads to Wiltshire towns
where you arrive in the afternoon and go home to firelit
tea through the autumn lanes, in a dog-cart. People in
detective stories catch the nine-something from Paddington. As for the Southern, with its trim green bourgeois
stations, all exactly alike, it is really just an extension of
the Underground, not a real railway at all.

But they are all pretty thin things compared with the
great sprawling, Promethean LMS, father of all railways,
whose high embankments, straddling the back gardens of
misty brick towns, are the bones of England. The LMS is
a piecemeal, empirical affair: it is organic, something that
developed from colliery tramways, long before this idea
of carrying *people* had taken root. You feel jolly lucky to be
allowed on an LMS train at all, when they have all these
iron bins to take to Northampton, these castings for
Houghton-le-Moors or Haltwhistle, these mild steel
flanges for J. Tonks, Acme Works, Engine-lane, Bloxwich.

The termini of other railways are straightforward and
rational; big glass halls with news theatres and flower
shops. Not so Euston, which is like a Midland warehouse,
littered with new bicycles half wrapped up in cardboard.
Indeed, I have a suspicion that Euston is also a market,
with regular auction sales of corrugated iron, and hens.
The heart of Euston is a kind of hall, with a few horse-hair
seats and a Victorian statue and ornate staircases—leading
doubtless, to board-rooms where consignors meet to
discuss loading regulations and tariffs, and corn chandlers
submit tenders for feeding all those LMS horses.

Departing passenger trains go from old, disused parts
of the market. Arrivals are met with an air of vexation.
Here's another of these passenger trains, they say, and
they make it wait for 20 minutes in that tunnel just outside

while they crossly remove the crates of bicycles from some obscure platform to make room for it.

Just outside Euston the lines converge into four simple tracks. It is very exciting to think that these open out into the whole clanking LMS system. This includes not only Crewe and Bootle but a great number of curious, dream-like places. There used to be, until this year, a notice in Coventry Station saying "Stations served by this railway. L to Q." Part of it ran:

Llanerchymedd. Llynclys. Long Buckby. Marple. Marple (Rose Hill). Marsh Gibbon and Poundon. Mochdre and Pabo. Moreton-in-March. Moreton-on-Lugg, Mumbles Road, Mumps. Mundesley-on-Sea.

The only one of these I have ever actually seen is Long Buckby, which is a reminder, even on the main London-Birmingham route, that the LMS is old enough to have many disused stations (Roade is another.) These are generally in black brick cuttings, with deserted, locked waiting-rooms and torn, 1924-ish advertisements flapping in the wind. Strangest of all, they are in the middle of rolling green meadows, with no sign of human habitation.

The whole list is an invaluable document for the economic historian, reminding us what bustling, import-ant places Mumps and Marsh Gibbon must have been when the LMS first came. We sigh for the vanished industries of Mumbles Road and Pabo, for the roaring days of Marple, when the prosperous new mill-owners built the pretty residential suburb of Rose Hill and petitioned for a separate station.

The LMS is probably the only one of the four that doesn't mind being called British Railways; for it *is* British, in the sense that Boadicea and Blake were. It communicates with the secret, inarticulate life of Britain;

with Rugeley, Staffs, with vasty moors, with places where they play football on Shrove Tuesday. It saw industry born, and it leads others in the old, wise melancholy knowledge that industry is not all. It will do its bit, of course. Now that the Government owns the mines and the railways no one on the LMS will be in the least surprised if trains suddenly plunge underground and emerge with six coal trucks hitched on behind. The LMS has seen everything before.

MOLASSES AND ALCOHOL

Until recently I had always thought of Epsom as just another of those North Downs places—the last bit of country before one gets to the misty brick valleys and water towers of South London. It is the sort of town one always observes, with faint surprise, on the way back, for it did not make much impression on the way out, in the sea-expectant morning. First the outskirts, the big detached 1905-ish houses with bricks very red and gables very white in the flat evening sunshine; then the town, with a comfortable-looking R.A.C. hotel, with hanging geraniums in a white portico; and the endless thwack-thwack of London-bound tyres. One thinks of Epsom people as connected with horses or retired.

Recently, however, I was *walking* through Epsom, and I saw, in the grounds of a big grey house under a green hill, a notice which said:

BOARD OF TRADE
DIRECTORATE OF MOLASSES AND
INDUSTRIAL ALCOHOL

At first sight this appears as arbitrary as a Directorate of Gin and Peas, or of Chocolate and Bacon. But really the incongruity is not in the actual juxtaposition. It may seem strange at first, this bracketing of fat, jolly, brown, bubbling molasses with thin, fiery, volatile, but somehow store-room-dreary industrial alcohol. But, as anyone will tell you who has looked at the textbooks of friends who went on with science after the School Certificate, when you get to *organic* chemistry everything seems to be made of various combinations of C, H and O, with little dotted-line boxes round the formulae; and it is no surprise to learn that industrial alcohol is in fact *made* from molasses, which is made from potatoes, mangolds and Jerusalem artichokes.

No, what stirs the imagination is the choice of Epsom. Molasses and industrial alcohol are both such unfinished, wholesale, raw-materialish things. One would expect a Directorate for them to be on the Mersey, or at Billing-ham-on-Tees. Perhaps Epsom was chosen as being neutral in a great rivalry between the North-East and the North-West of England. One somehow connects real, natural molasses with the West Indies and piccaninnies. One imagines, in the roaring nineteenth century, the distinc-tive, bulbous molasses boats coming in to Liverpool; the dockers' disputes over "sticky money"; the four-horse drays with bins of molasses rumbling off from the docks to the tall warehouse in Engine-lane. All this Jerusalem artichoke business belongs, like soya beans and plastics, to a later period, when organic chemistry had really got going.

How secure the molasses magnates must have felt, in their Cheshire mansions, while all the time a young unknown chemist was busy in a shed outside Doncaster with an evil-smelling heap of fermenting mangolds. Soon impersonal new brick factories would spring up all along the East Coast, producing alcohol in unheard-of quantities from Lincolnshire and Lowlands potatoes. The Liverpool magnates rationalise their fleets, send chemists to Jamaica to make the alcohol out there and reduce freight costs. Rivalry increases, right up to the recent war. Then Whitehall invites both sides to a meeting. A very stormy meeting. The permanent Civil Servants exchange meaning glances as the business men thump the table, monotonously advancing the claims of Billingham and Bootle.

A week later the great convoy assembles at the Board of Trade, Millbank, S.W.1. The lorries are loaded with those dreary Civil Service tables on iron trestles, with the files on Fractionation Statistics and the Molasses Bending Index; with the principals' carpets; with easels and drawing boards from the Welfare Section, half-finished posters graphically showing an absent-minded worker falling into a vat of molasses. One sees it all—the advance party arranging billets; the initial suspicion of the Epsom people, the get-together dances; the chatty, Roneo'd office magazine, doubtless called *Epsom Salts* ("We hear that Maisie, of Treacle Liaison Typing Pool, is not so anxious to go home to London these week-ends. Ask a certain trainer. . . .")

A more sinister explanation is possible. Perhaps the organic chemists have gone even further and discovered how to make industrial alcohol directly from gorse and bracken, by-passing molasses altogether; and perhaps these people at Epsom are secretly preparing for a kind of home groundnuts scheme, with a grand assault on the Surrey commons for their raw materials.

I hope not. It will take even longer to drive out of London.

PATRIOT RAISES
UGLY HEAD

This poem
Is for people who rave about French films. It will show
    'em
That there is at least one person who does not think it
    logical
To say a love-story is necessarily subtle, tense, profound or
    psychological
Merely because the man and the wench
Are both French.
La Bête Humaine
Is the sort of film that makes you forget Pascal, Racine
    Corneille and Taine

And convinces you that the word "Gallic"
Is synonymous with "phallic."
It is possible that when lovers are closeted
A woman *likes* to have her lips bitten and be similarly
    cossetted
But on the screen
This is obscene:
And Jean Gabin
Is just another indication that the *siècle* has reached its *fin:*
I do not believe, with him and Ernest Hemingway,
That the flow of civilised European conversation since
    Jane Austen should be stemmed in—well, in such a
    stemming way:
It seems such a waste
For the accumulated elegance of complex diction to be
    replaced
By monosyllabic grunts,
Meaningful sideways looks, and long wordless scenes in
    punts.
The only point
Where I laughed, in a solitary way (for the Curzon is a
    sniffy joint)
Was when Gabin said "To night
I have the courage to kill your husband," (the first time
    he took fright)
And she said "Not to night. Oh no,"
In a bored way that suggested they already had tickets for
    a show.
I do not believe that all the citizens of France
Plan murders as casually as we plan going to a dance
But it really isn't odd
If these doleful irrelevant murders, the husband like a sad
    cod,

The naive French pride
In that railway engine on which the camera has such a
    long ride,
The dance at which chain-smoking mechanics and women
    who are definitely rather scrawny
Gyrate to waltz tunes which can only be described as corny
Make one suspect that if this had come from Rank
People would say it stank.

ENGINEERING SPIRITS

In these days it is rather difficult for humanity to retain any feeling for those numinous presences which in previous ages have given meaning to the world. There are no dryads in St. John's Wood and Pan does not inhabit Arnos Grove. Yet this is only because our conception of numina is out of date. It requires a highly cultivated awareness and tranquillity to apprehend the spirits of a vanished age of agricultural rhythms. We may perhaps just catch a suggestion of the subliminal, only just existing spirit of a bridge, brooding at evening over its black water; but generally this sort of thing requires the cosmic dreaming of a Yeats.

Let us forget fairies and come to our own day and age.
We are surrounded by spirits and sub-souls if we only take
the trouble to look. Who can be in a bus, for instance,
without seeing at once that it moves as a unity; there must
be some simpler principle than all those rods and wheels
between the engine and the back axle. Is not a bus
informed by some harmless, genial, but somehow *lumbering*
spirit? A bus has the kind of spirit which, if spirits went
to school, would be overgrown and unclever, sitting at the
back of the class whittling spiritual sticks and bursting out
of spiritual clothes, but later growing up to do its large,
reliable job in an uncomplaining way which makes the
more volatile spirits—the spirits, say, of printing machines
or helicopters—feel in some way guilty and over-sophis-
ticated.

Consider the melancholy spirit of a tram, caught in
tragic ambiguity trying to give unity to a vehicle which
appears to be straining to move simultaneously from both
ends. And how shall we apprehend the differing atmos-
pheres of steam trains and tube trains unless we are aware
of the fierce, masculine, bustling but slightly Micawberish
spirit that informs a locomotive, drawing those calm
female carriages who refuse to be impressed by his
prowess when he snortles into the terminus—for have
they not their own maternal function, bringing forth
renewed passengers on to the platform of life?

The tube train, on the other hand, has a very low level
of consciousness, not identified with any part of itself but
distributed throughout its entire length—a kind of worm-
soul. You could cut a tube train in half and it wouldn't
mind.

To each age its own spirits. That seems an elementary
rule, yet it seems to have escaped notice that by far the

most easily observable of all modern spirits are those nimble elementals of the air aptly called atmospherics.

Mere radio experts assert that atmospherics have something to do with sunspots. They say, too, that you can't include the hoarse gabbling voices in the bottom right-hand corner of the loud-speaker, the demented, squeaky orchestras playing down at the other end of a long iron pipe, the submarine choirs singing their jerky oratorios in short, regular pulses, among real atmospherics. They limit the term to those demon cacklings and moon wailings, to that scrabbling sound which suggests a huge paw, ten feet in diameter, appearing gropingly over the wall of a county lunatic asylum on a clear summer day. Cold-bloodedly, they try to make a dry scientific selection and classification of all the sounds which cut so disconcertingly across one's Mozart. The atmospherics that have voices, they say, are merely real human stations distorted.

Well, I don't believe them. On internal evidence I don't believe them; for in America, where they think to have escaped from the sad fountains and groves of Europe, these radio experts betray their real limitations by calling atmospherics "static". Imagine, static! On my radio, it is the real programme that is static, by comparison with these atmospherics. No modern symphony, no Cup Final commentary, no *human* broadcast can match the frenzy of my atmospherics on a really good psychic night.

If these manifestations are only human stations distorted, why can't one turn the knob just a little farther and *get* the human station, eh? Because atmospherics bound away, squeaking with tinny laughter, from unbelievers and scientists. Nor will it do to conduct painstaking research in the manner of the late Mr. Harry Price. You just have to *accept* atmospherics, and once you do, it is an easy step to most of the other elementals. It is a mistake to think that spirits belong only to ponds and solitudes. This clicking, banging, whirring modern world is much more to the liking of your true, volatile Ariel than all the bucolic centuries from which he is at last freed.

WESTERN LAW (1)

One of the paradoxes of the age of speed is that it is still difficult to believe in motion at all. We look at the top deck of a bus; we see the passengers, with solemn faces like the stylised men in cartoons, divided into arbitrary couples, uneasily aware of each other's existence; and we have a sudden intuition of the absurdity of this prim arm-chair motion ten feet above the ground. We see them, as it were, without the bus. Even the nautical expression "top deck," with its suggestion of life-boats and spray, carries with it a dim European racial memory of the original Greek moving thing, the ship, cleaving the violet waters, already looked upon rather doubtfully in the famous *Antigone* chorus as a slightly bumptious human attempt to lord it over space.

We begin to realise what Zeno meant when he pointed out that a moving arrow must, at any moment, actually *be* in some place, so it can't really be moving at all. It seems even more unlikely that the people in that curious elevated waiting-room should be moving. We still live in and are formed by the English countryside, which was created by men with the mental speed-limit of an ambling horse: we see it through the eyes of Cobbett.

It is this implicit realisation of the tension between real life, weighty with the centuries, and the unreal motor bus that makes the Bristol Omnibus Services Time-table, Regulations and Conditions such an absorbing document. The world of mellifluous English villages—Peasedown, Hinton Charterhouse, Limpley Stoke—the world of County Assizes and old inns and immemorial grazing rights, brings all its sense of ancient precedent and custom to bear on this robot intrusion, carefully hedging it about with human bye-laws, absorbing it into civilisation. The very names of the constituent companies suggest these two worlds; for they are the Bristol Tramways and Carriage Co., Ltd., the Bath Electric Tramways, Ltd., and Bath Tramways Motor Co., Ltd. Bath and Bristol may stand as allegorical types of the two elements in modern England, evenly balanced, mutually tolerant, but for ever different; industrial and traditional—one might almost say, on a lower plane, Conservative and Socialist.

It is still just possible to associate counterparts of Jane Austen's young ladies, on their way to visit friends at very good lodgings in Milsom-street, with the Bath Electric Tramways. One sees the highly varnished tram, adorned with the city arms, its top deck uncovered, trundling on a timeless summer day past dignified shops with blinds that say "Estd. 1763." But Bristol, with its aeroplane factories and hilly brick suburbs, is a very different matter. The Bristol element is obviously responsible for other place names in the Timetable, such as Cable Works, Hortham Colony, Leyhill Prison, and Air Balloon (not *The* Air Balloon; just Air Balloon, it says), which all sound like part of some inhuman Kafka landscape.

It is indeed a mixed company with which the Bristol Omnibus Services must deal. What happens when a busload of ladies on their way to the Women's Institute at Lulsgate Bottom or Compton Dando is disturbed by some of these terrible Hortham Colonists, or by Leyhill Prisoners, or even by strange Martian creatures from Air Balloon pushing down the gangway? What do *they* care about bye-laws? After all, we should expect persons who hold Scholar's or Apprentice's Tickets travelling home for the holidays to nod equably and pay the extra when the Conductor reads Regulation 6(f) which says that such tickets are not available on Sundays and Bank Holidays; or even, if they were in a party, as Scholars or Apprentices might well be, returning noisily from the Choir Outing or a visit to an unusual gasworks, to obey on request Regulation 2(1)xiv, forbidding them to "throw any article from the vehicle or attach to or trail from the vehicle any streamer, balloon, flag or other article."

Apprentices have brawled in the streets and Scholars have had their fling ever since medieval Paris; turn the page and they are furred aldermen and chirurgeons. But what of these others? The bye-laws include them too, in a common humanity; but to treat of so vast an enterprise in the space at our command would defeat the nimblest pen. We shall deal with the matter in fuller measure in an ensuing article.

Pray REFRAIN from Spitting

WESTERN LAW (2)

In our last article, examining the Bristol Omnibus Services Timetable, Regulations and Conditions, we saw how this work may fairly claim to be the type or mode of all English motor transport bye-laws, a common legal bond subsuming the traditional, as represented by Bath, and the functional or industrial, as represented by Bristol. We saw how the buses might expect not only villagers from Much Marcle, or Dead Maids, or Charmy Down, or Madam's End, but also potentially lawless immigrant workers from Chittening Trading Estate, miners from the old condemned village of Coalpit Heath; or taciturn technocrats from the squat mysterious plant, ugly concrete blocks behind barbed wire on the dunes, at Sea Mills. (Perhaps the best single example of one route containing both elements is No. 307—Downend (Horseshoe), Blackhorse, Folly, New Engine, Kendleshire Turn and Coalpit Heath.) Now let us examine the consummate skill with which all these diverse populations are placed on an equal legal footing.

In the Regulations three main approaches are combined, with masterly effect. We may summarise these as Technical Wonder, Contract, and Description.

Technical Wonder is used to bring all passengers to a proper sense of amazed gratitude that there should be a regular bus service at all. "The Companies hereby give notice" (and that goes for you, too, New Engineers) "that they do not undertake, nor . . . are they to be deemed to undertake that their Public Service Vehicles shall operate on service at the time specified in their Time Table, *or at all*" (my italics) ". . . or be accountable for any loss, damage, hurt, inconvenience or injury arising from the failure of the vehicles to start or arrive at the time specified in their Time Table or at all. . . ." It is difficult to see how anybody could be hurt by the failure of a vehicle to *start;* but the bye-lawyers evidently imagined some such scene as the following, on a cold morning.

The driver, worn out with attempts to start the engine, is leaning panting against the radiator. A knowall from New Engine gets out irritably and says "Mixture's too rich, mate," and insists on having a turn himself. The great engine backfires and the handle breaks his wrist. Well, it's not a bit of good *his* asking for compensation. He should have left everything to the omniscient Companies, with their wise foreknowledge that

there are some days when Things simply resist men. They
know, too, that the forces of nature are not to be treated
disrespectfully; there is an air of placatory sacrifice, of
the primitive appeasement of daemonic forces, about the
Companies' refusal of responsibility for an accident "on
any Toll-bridge, Ferry or other transport across water."
Down in the West Country, where estuaries bring quiet
arms of the sea in among the green fields, they know that
water is not to be trusted.   The ferry, a practically
circular boat, with old-fashioned reciprocating engines
and a tall thin funnel, may *look* industrial enough, but the
drivers and conductors know better.   They stop their
ears against the seductive voices of the water-maidens
and the half-heard music from Atlantis. They never really
relax until the bus is bumping off the gangway again in
bottom gear.

Technical Wonder having thus established the emo-
tional or affective background, we are ready for the intellectual argument, the element of Contract.   As the
name implies, Contract is the enfranchisement of every
passenger, whether he be rich or so lowly that "his
condition is such as to be offensive to passengers" in a
great system of rights and duties.   For instance, "If a
passenger holding a return ticket desires to return by
railway . . . he will, on presenting such ticket at a railway
station, be given the opportunity of entering into a contract with the railway executive entitling him to return
by train." We see the man who has missed the last bus
back from Weston-super-Mare being shown into the
deserted station.   Gradually the lights go up all over the
place as clerical staff are called on duty. The man is shown
into a room furnished with a desk, leather armchairs and
high bookcases.   He rings up his lawyer, who presently

arrives, and they all get down to business with the railway lawyers. Telephone calls are made to the railway executive in London, documents are signed and stamped. Everything is codified, every emergency is legally catered for.

The third element, Description, is the purely literary side of the Regulations, bringing to life with Dickensian skill the multifarious passengers. In this vast human panorama there are people who contemptuously "spit upon the Vehicle," people who "wilfully remove notice boards, fare tables" and even "number plates"; people who "when in or on the Vehicle," suddenly "throw money in the road or footway:" they "beg, sell, or offer articles for sale"; they clamber on with "Accumulators, Dangerous or Offensive Goods and Materials, Loaded Firearms" and, of course, the inevitable "Folding Push Chairs." They are indeed a diverse crowd. But the Regulations are ready for them.

LINISHERS, BANDSAWS AND QUINCHING TANKS

What fun it would be one of these Tuesday mornings, while coal trains are clanking busily over yellow brick suburbs, while Oaths are being Commissioned in basement offices over cups of cold lawyer's tea, while the great tram and mangle factories south of the river are in full blast, to leave London and go to one of the auctions of plant and machinery that are always being advertised on the upper levels of the Underground!

It is only on the District and Metropolitan Lines that you see these lists, laid out in heavy type like playbills. On the deeper levels of the tube the people, nearly all bound for Piccadilly, are thought worthy of only the more frivolous advertisements. They have to be shown the way to Waterloo or Paddington by coloured lights. Indeed they even have to be directed TO THE TRAINS, or they would probably wander fecklessly into some sad, dripping grotto, or a secret underground factory, or get lost in dark halls full of bats where Things, with a damp chuckle, vanish down endless corridors.

But on the upper levels, with their quiet, wooden— platformed, aquatint stations, illumined for short periods of the day by dusty sunbeams filtering over high blank walls, it is different. There is an air of purposeful, Victorian mercantilism. The passengers are sober people, assumed to be interested in things like the NOTICE OF SEA SURCHARGES, from which may be learnt the cost of sending a corpse to Northern Ireland. Most of all, it is assumed that they want to buy machinery.

It never seems to be quite ordinary machinery. Here is a typical list:

> Gang-slitting and Abrasive Cutting-off Machines. Arc and Spot Welders. 25,000 Pressed Steel Wheels. Drawings, Work-in-Progress and Materials for Potato-peelers and Lawn-mowers.

The only normal things here are the welders. One asks oneself what kind of a business it was. First they instal this brutal gang-slitting machine. They make these 25,000 wheels. Then they abandon lawn-mowers, probably when they get to the difficult bit, the blades (I expect my lawn-mower, which always wants to cut straight down into the earth, was made by these people),

H

which sound easier. No wonder they are having an auction.

The lists seem to be aimed at marginal industrialists rather than great firms who have standing orders for boiler replacement, and just call in an architect when they want to build a factory extension. One thinks of individuals, young men putting new life into inherited, moribund family businesses, small paper-mills or panel-beating works; men without many industrial contacts, men who have been wondering for weeks where they could get a good cheap Belt and Triple Drum Sander; men still in touch with the life of small country towns; men, even, with an ear for poetry.

For the lists are always compiled with a splendid cumulative rhythm. For example:

> Wadkin Radial and Fixed Head Routers. Centreless Cutter Tap and Cutter Grinders. Wheeling, Folding and Rolling Machines by Herbert.

Observe the controlled increase in complexity of imagery—the stark, blunt "Wadkin Radial"; then the Hegelian negatives, the clash of ideas, in the second line; the sudden lovely, liquid leaping into life of "Wheeling, Folding and Rolling Machines by Herbert". Here the poet has a bold vision of Sir Alfred Herbert as a modern counterpart of the maker of Pinocchio, the puppet who came to life. One sees these machines, in the moonlit factory, wheeling, folding and rolling all by themselves to a strange, Honegger-like music.

Sometimes there is tragedy, the list telling its own story of an old-established business being squeezed out of existence. Take this, for instance:

> Heaters, Pulpers, Stuff Chests. Rag or Straw Boilers. Reeling and Cutting Machines. Water Wheels and

Turbine Electric Generators. 15-ton Road Weighbridge. 18 Dwelling Houses.

One can see the whole history of the firm. First, the
days of the Jacobean Stuff Chests; then old Hezekiah,
the real father of the business, installing the water wheel
in 1751; the quarrels with his grandson over the new-
fangled reeling and cutting machines. Here is the sepia
photograph of a bowler-hatted, moustachioed drayman
standing by the new weighbridge in 1892, here the group
taken nearly thirty years later, when the turbine electric
generators were installed, the workers from the eighteen
dwelling houses afterwards being entertained by the
management.

One hopes they will find the right kind of buyer—some
jolly Cheeryble brothers, who will take over the whole
lot and run the business as before. And where will such be
found, if not on the Metropolitan Railway?

UTILITY CONCERT

Well,
Musicians never *did* look very swell,
And I expect these variously-shaped ladies in black, with
      Peter Pan collars,
These thin men who are sitting down with their trombones,
Palely joking among the tuning-up moans
Cannot be said to look like a million dollars
Since they have probably worked all day at a lathe, or a
      desk, or at monging fish:
I expect when they start
Their celestial art
Will waft me as near to heaven as I could wish.

Here comes the soloist
In a black velvet gown and a Metropolitan aura:
She smiles at the applause which is her due
(It never seems to baura)
And poises her hands for the opening of the Brahms
    Number Two. . . .

In recent years
The inner tension I used to feel at the sight of a French
    horn
Has abated somewhat, though there are still fears
That this instrument lugubrious and forlorn
Will bubble, or fill with saliva, or do one of its usual things
In the middle of some tender dialogue with the strings.
This time it really *does* let us down
With hesitant glugging noises that make even the pianist
    frown.

The tympani are taken
By a lady who is evidently determined to earn her bacon:
She watches the beat with the grimness of one about to
    hang
So that instead of coming in with the *tutti*—BANG—
She wins by a short head
And we have BER-bang instead.
Her sister on the cymbals, as a kind of compensation,
With very un-Bacchic deliberation
Begins the inward motion of her hands
At the very moment when the beat demands
A splendid crash, and her contribution, though great,
Is always late.
Although I admit their devotion to Art
Why can't they stick to Beethoven and Mozart

If the irregular rhythms of the Later Romantics
Produce such antics?
Moreover, there are several sins
Among the first violins
Who seem to think they need only play the right notes
For fierce Beauty to grip us all by our throats:
It is as though they had left a saucepan of milk on the boil
And were afraid it might spoil.
If I should say to the sorriest fellow
"What adjective would you apply to the cello
(Apart from yellow)?"
He would almost bellow
"Mellow",

And, indeed, I should be soothed by their sonority
If, being only two, they were not in such a minority.
If this were all, I could have borne it—
But now I perceive a man with a CORNET.
That's torn it!

THE BEE-SMUGGLERS

One of the sumptuary industries which we all welcomed
back after the war was tourism. Those posters, those little
pamphlets, those mushrooming travel agencies, were all
happy signs that life was expanding again, that once
again we should dance in the orchards and sip our wine
on the sunlit terraces, as Europeans have always done.
And yet, as the atomic age rolls on, we begin to have an
uneasy suspicion that travel is not the carefree thing it was.
It all seems to be mixed up with a hustling kind of
commerce. Even the nationalised airlines, by a curious
paradox, address their advertisements to the sort of bluff
tycoon whom this country has not seen since the Rand

gold discoveries; he is constantly adjured to fly to remote
and unexploited countries and conclude vast deals with
persons who are represented as equally impatient of letter-
writing and all the respectable trappings of traditional
commerce.

Even "popular" tourist literature is unconsciously
affected by this utilitarian outlook. A good example is
provided by a little booklet called *South Africa In a Nutshell*.
This begins, just like any pre-war booklet, with the words,
"The broad, colourful canvas that is South Africa spreads
far beyond the limitations of a *Nutshell* publication . . ."
and most if it is nice easy reading about history, motoring,
coastal resorts, and so on, all written in terms of the
average visitor. And then, suddenly, without any warning
of a change in tempo, the reader is confronted with an
extraordinary List of Prohibited Articles. These include:

> Bees, honey, second-hand hives; substances containing
>   honey, including those attached to fly-papers, etc.
> Broomcorn and articles made from broom derived from
>   sorghum.
> Carbide of calcium.
> Certain knives.
> Dead bodies.
> Foods, including mealie products, pulses, prunes.
> Linoleum, gasketting, sashcord and furnishing fabrics, bags,
>   pockets or woolpacks.
> Leather, adulterated.
> Opium pipes.
> Prison-made goods.
> Sausage casings.
> Second-hand articles, including rags.
> Unmounted artificial teeth.
> Uranium.

It's incredible. Who *are* these people, with their
medieval woolpacks, their obsession with the second-hand,

their curious alternation between the rag-and-bone trade and the sort of traffic that is discussed at Geneva conventions—uranium, opium? For we may assume that no one could have *invented* a list like this unless he were a poet. This latter is, indeed, an interesting hypothesis. One imagines the list in some Walt Whitman saga about the fruits of the earth:

> I see you, you cunning adulterators of leather, you prison-workers making your goods,
> And you, my brothers that toil in the heaving cities, making sausage casings, unmounted artificial teeth and certain knives,
> You Flemings, you Huguenots with your woolpacks, I salute you, I am your brother. . . .

but we must abandon this, with regret, in favour of the more obvious explanation—that all travellers are now commercial travellers. That list was compiled by South African customs men with bitter experience of the same scene, endlessly repeated. The harmless-looking tourist family, with dark glasses and cameras, is waiting in the customs sheds at Cape Town. "What's in that?" says the official, pointing to a large crate. "Oh, just clothes and things," says the "father" airily. But the official, wearily opening it, is not surprised to find it bulging with second-hand hives and opium pipes. A white-coated chemist comes out from his special dockside laboratory with one of the pile of hides which the "mother" has brazenly declared. "Just as I thought," he says, "it's adulterated—only 10 per cent, is leather. The rest is——" (what *could* it be? How do you adulterate leather?). Even the "child," when compelled to take off his dark glasses, turns out to be a dwarf representing a shady firm of mealie product manufacturers.

Even on this hypothesis it is difficult to account for some of the items. Broomcorn, for instance, and broom derived from sorghum. Sorghum has a splendid geography-book authenticity as something that South Africa abounds in already, 50 trains a day reaching the cities and ports from the great sorghum mines, or sorghum plantations, or sorghum refineries. People with the commercial acumen of those smuggler-tourists would never dream of bringing in *more* sorghum to such a buyers' market.

And what about those terrible dead bodies? Could these be the corpses of accomplices smuggling uranium, killed on the boat by radio-activity or Russian spies? It is too alarming to consider, on a holiday at any rate. I don't want to be mixed up in it. I am sorry to disappoint the travel agencies, but I think I shall just go to Frinton-on-Sea.

THE WALGERS

Readers of daily newspapers these days are justified in expecting to find all the apocalyptic news—the solemn walkings-out at Lake Success, the hydrogen bomb and soon, doubtless, the even more terrible litmus bomb—on the left-hand side of the front page, under the main headline. One somehow expects the right-hand side to be more domestic and recognisable; even, at intervals, comfortable.

It was, therefore, very disconcerting a few days ago to read on the *right*-hand side of a London evening paper this story:

LONDON BOY GANGSTERS WARNED

Mr. Frank Powell, the Clerkenwell magistrate, to-day warned members of a gang of youths who, it was said, were "upsetting" clubs in North London.

LATEST

CENTRAL 30000

HUGE EXPLOSIONS ACCOMPANY SUNSPOTS

TOKIO, Thursday.—Sunspots observed from here have been accompanied by tremendous explosions, Japanese astronomers said to-day.—Reuter.

He had been told that after a gang had smashed windows and furniture at a school in Killick Street, King's Cross, last night, police saw 50 to 70 youths walging in Caledonian Road. . . .

This would be a perfect item to inclose in a Time Capsule selection of information for posterity about our contemporary unease. It begins, reasonably enough, with the reassuring words "Clerkenwell magistrate." We know where we are, so far. We see the bench, the policemen, the ordered processes of law, the carefully preserved European *mores*. It is but a short step from this to the city guilds, to the medieval minds at work on Roman Law, to our snug nest of civilisation. Nor do we yet feel the problem of "a gang of youths" to be an insoluble one. There have always been gangs of youths. True, we are to some extent responsible for these particular gangs. *We* had the Industrial Revolution, *we* built the Wen; but we can cope with this, the earth is still under our feet.

The first hint of chaos and dissolution comes with the sudden, breathless interruption from Tokio. We are whisked from the sober, oak-panelled, almost cosy police-court into the clear bright light of some futuristic play. We are uncomfortably aware of the relevance to us all of what Professor Ishiboshi, his eye glued to the telescope, excitedly reports in twittering, bird-like Japanese, to the listening Doctor Matsodusti. In our hearts we feel that when the world does end it will be announced from Japan. . . .

Restraining the urge to telephone Central 30000 and ask what the Home Office arrangements for sunspot emergencies are, we try to focus our attention on Clerkenwell again. But the old familiarity has gone. We have a sense of old forms twisted into a strange new life; it is like listening to Prokofiev's Classical Symphony after Mozart. For we are soon up against something terrible and new on our own door-step. Unmistakably, in the middle of the Caledonian-road, there are these fifty to seventy youths walging.

Well may the police have been alarmed at the dreadful sight. They could deal with shouted insults, with stone-throwing, with rioting even. But this—this horrible blind, corporate movement, half-way between bulging and waltzing, this mute, resistless pressure, welling out-wards from a half-formed, lubberly totemic dance, deaf to reason—there is no precedent for walging. We imagine the Commissioner scanning the reports as they come into the station. He gets up from his chair and stares out over the London roofs. "Fifty to seventy," he murmurs. "It's come at last." He remembers his childhood, the secret group on the asphalt play-ground, the cracked bell, the lawlessness barely contained. A nerve twitches in his head. He walks over to a large map of London. Chalked underneath on the blackboard strip is the legend, WALGING. CORRECT TO 1200 HRS. MARCH 5. He stares at it for a moment. Then, wearily, he lifts the receiver. . . .

DREAMING STAIRS

I can think of no situation in London life so anaesthetic to the ordinary processes of thought as being on an UP escalator. For millions, this is the everyday equivalent of that timeless dream in which Mr T. S. Eliot's elegant but tortured characters spend so much of their lives:

You are not the same people who left that station
Or who will arrive at any terminus:
While the narrowing rails slide together behind you
And on the deck of the drumming liner
You shall not say "the past is finished"
Or "the future is before us".

It is just the same on the drumming escalator. Time is suspended. It is, as Boethius would have put it, duration without succession. The endless advertisements float before our unseeing eyes, leaving no impression save a vague general notion of female accoutrements. Our thoughts become less and less practical, more and more speculative as we move dreamily upwards, like pre-Raphaelite angels on our way to a mild, cloudy plateau. We step off in an abstraction.

Our preliminary recall to reality is the discovery, at the top, that the escalator has a name. "Waygood-Otis," it says on the comb thing. Now that is a fine, reassuring name for an escalator. It sounds big and international, like Metro-Vickers and Mond Nickel, and also sophisticated and cosmopolitan, like Waldorf-Astoria. (It seems strange that those creaking, antique lifts, where the gates always crash open on the side that you aren't, were also make by these Waygood-Otis people.) You would expect to find a cast-iron plate saying: "Huggins and Bostock, Bros. (Bootle), Hydraulic Platform Factors." But this is not a very practical thought; we are still far away, ill-prepared for the rough demand for tickets and the clamour of the streets.

This is probably because, fundamentally, we have not got over our amazement at these wonderful stairs that so magically relieve us of all responsibility. There is still something of the Ideal Homes Exhibition about escalators. What will they think of next? Confused, not too technical explanations occur to us. Sometimes we can see lights between the buckets. So there must be men underneath there, in a very peculiar-shaped room. Do they have their machinery in a vast triangular chamber, of which the escalator is the hypotenuse? Or is it a sort of *banana-*

I

shaped room? It requires quite an effort of the imagination to imagine the whole thing bending round the other way: it is like trying to think of a circle inside-out, or the square root of minus one.

It is just this hiddenness of the machinery which gives the escalator its eerie charm. There are no brakesmen with levers, no clanging bells, no bright steam engines, no slightest indication of how it is done; just this miraculous supply of buckets, issuing endlessly forth as though they had just been made—anonymous, not caring whether it is the rush hour or the doldrums. Late at night, in deserted outlying stations you may hear the escalator rumbling, squeaking and gibbering all alone, as though it contemplated throwing out an extra, snaky length of itself, swallowing up the ticket machines and any stray passengers, and chewing them up into a horrid mincemeat. There is also an obscure association with dredgers. The escalator is surely developed from the dredger, a clanking useful thing that must have been invented before such a luxurious, citified apparatus. Perhaps the escalators do become dredgers at night emptying the Tube of slimy, green water.

Fear of being dredged or minced, however, is not really dominant on the UP escalator. Nor are we really afraid that the governors on the machinery will one day break down, so that the buckets fly upwards at twenty miles an hour and we are flung off at the top by sheer centrifugal force. We are in too much of a trance to be afraid, or to take seriously the notice which says: *A fixed staircase is provided for passengers not desirous of using the escalator*.

It is different, however, on the DOWN, where we are on a conveyor belt into the unknown. We are fully prepared, alert, even suspicious. We are on the defensive, ready to choose the right corridor. Subconsciously we are relieved that mechanical arms do not come down and screw stoppers on our heads, or scrub us, or wrap labels round us, as in some Donald Duck fantasy.

Consciously, we are afraid of falling flat on our faces.

FOOD FLASH

"Fadge and Bacon"—a Ministry Of Food recipe

Everybody is rude
About the Ministry of Food,
So let me explain at the beginning, I don't think it Marxian
    or sinister,
While Food is scarce, to entrust it to a Ministry, with a
    Minister;
It is not politics, but imagination, possibly mistaken,
Which tells me I could never like fadge and bacon.
Fadge
Sounds like something shaken off a spoon, falling on to the
    plate in a wodge (or wadge);
I have an instant grudge
Against this substance that sounds halfway between mash and
    fudge;
Just as only in a sheet do I appreciate the quality of sheet-ness
So do I shrink from spoiling my nice crisp bacon with this
    fadge, because of its out-of-place, turnipy sweetness.
No, I will drain the post-war cup to the dregs;
I will stick to bacon and no eggs.

HOUSEHOLD NOISES

The death last week of the founder and chairman of
Boddery Household Noises recalls one of the most romantic
commercial careers of modern times. In 1923 Alfred
Boddery, young and unknown, was joke editor in a small
matchbox firm, where his inventive mind was bringing
him more frustration than advancement. To many men
the job would have been satisfying enough; but in between
reading the proofs of his jokes, seeing lawyers about copy-
right, and running down to the printers, Boddery realised
that he was in a "blind alley" occupation. Whenever he
had a really progressive idea, such as that of having
interminable serial jokes so that the public would buy
his firm's matches to see the ending, the management
turned it down.

Boddery used to say in later years that he owed the

idea which brought him success to his wife. As he was leaving his house with her one night she went back to switch on the hall light, for she shared with many others the conviction that to burglars this would denote occupation and thus keep them away. When Boddery pointed out that all burglars knew that trick, she laughingly retorted: "Why don't you invent a trick they don't know?"

He accepted the challenge, and the result was Boddery's original Thumping Machine—in principle a large box with a sounding-board; an interior mechanism caused the four thumping arms to beat against this, so that when the machine was left running in an unoccupied house it conveyed the impression of a constant procession up and down the stairs.

The Thumping Machine was an instant success. But Boddery laid the foundations of Household Noises not so much by his salesmanship and advertising, excellent though these were, as by the ingenuity with which he always kept one step ahead of the thinking burglar. The latter soon realised that all the bangs and thumps coming from empty houses were unaccompanied by the sound of any human voice. So Boddery brought out his "Merry Cries" record. The reverse side of this contained the famous One-sided Telephone Conversation. Another popular early line was the Boddery Meal Simulator, a device in which knives, forks, and spoons, suspended from a pulley system, gave a realistic imitation of a hearty meal in progress.

Household Noises rapidly expanded into a major domestic industry. The 1930 advertisement reproduced opposite gives an idea of the remarkable progress made in seven short years.

No scientific development was overlooked by Boddery.

Up to his death he was working on new techniques in invisible ray remote control. Last week I was shown over the Household Noises exhibit for this year's Ideal Home Exhibition, in which Boddery had taken a personal interest. As I approached a model house it was wrapped in a ghostly, dark silence. But when I got to within twenty yards and crossed a hidden ray which activated a selenium cell mechanism, the whole place suddenly burst into amazing life. I could have sworn there were three families there. One was singing glees in a front room, another was having an uproarious party somewhere at the back, a third was playing some mysterious game which involved running up and down the stairs.

A child was doing a bit of fretwork, and someone else was on the telephone. Dogs barked, babies squealed, people played "The Rustle of Spring" and gargled, and

there was someone having a bath. Life was being lived very fully and richly in that house.

It may be long before such luxuries are available to the home market, for, as a Board of Trade spokesman said last week, Boddery's products are in high demand in America and the dollar countries. It is a fitting tribute to this prince of gadgeteers.

PSYCHOTYPING

It always gives me quite a shock when I see typists typing and realise that they *aren't looking at the keys*. It seems incredible. I can remember the top row, qwertyuiop, because that is a kind of word; you can pronounce it. It would be quite a good ononmatopoeic word for corkscrew, *qwe – rt* being the squeaky noise of the cork turning round and *yui – OP* being it coming out. But asdfghjkl, although fairly memorable, is too confusing with "a" and "s" so arbitrarily added to the alphabetical sequence. And as for zxcvbnm—I don't see how anybody could remember that.

Some time ago I asked one of these no-look typists how she did it. She said they began by typing that thing about the quick brown fox, slowly. Well, I tried it slowly and I got this remarkable poem:

```
th quoci
The quick briwn fox jiumoec the quock bobrow
the quock bo
the qi
the quicj brown hox ji ji jumoef over the lazu fod
the quoci
thr quo
the quick brown fox jumpeffed over the lazu llazy
fdodfdoh dodof f dof doh doh dog.
```

I realised straight away that I have remarkable gifts as a typewriter medium. These ordinary typists, by a rigid mechanical discipline, have imposed their conscious will on the machine, making it write dreary orders for spange-ing irons, and thursling rods, and copper and silk stone grummets. But the typewriter takes me straight into the collective unconscious of the West. Jung says somewhere that the nightmare, the fire-breathing horse that sym-bolised terror for pre-industrial man, is being replaced by locomotives or great black machines out of control. So, too, the typewriter replaces the planchette, the sybil, or the inspired idiot as the mouthpiece of these verbal race memories. We do not know yet what the *quock bobrow*, or even the *quock bo*, is. The typewriter throws up these disturbing concepts for our consideration and then goes off into a counter-melody in the scat-singing idiom (*ji ji jumoef*); then there is a return to this *quoc* motif, or arche-type. The last line produces a splendid verb, *jumpeff*—so much stronger than mere "jump". It suggests the fox (or *hox*) sailing insolently over the *lazu fdodfdoh*, going "*pff*" contemptuously as it does so. Yet this marvellous extension and exploration of language is all done in the medium of a popular song, like Edith Sitwell's earlier verse. I should like to hear Danny Kaye sing that last line.

It is fairly clear, however, that the typewriter is trying to come through with some basic message about the *quoci*. A little patient work by a trained analyst would soon straighten it out. But it is not always so simple. The typewriter taps such a rich, teeming world that several attempts often disclose no unity to the layman. Consider, for instance, these two versions of a well-known poem:

> matu laf a lyytle lamv
> id gleece was qgite as sbei
> abd evertwhere that maty wabt
> that lamh was stee to ho.

> maty gas a lyyrrlr lavm pamb lanm
>   labm lamn lamh ba blast
> utd forrcr aa waa whire as svie
> abd everytgwee ygar maty webt
> yhat la, j waa sure yo go

> kank lamj nub b b b lamn lamb
>   575757575

How *European* this is! What lyrical variations are called up by the tender associations of "little"—the charming Anglo-Saxon *lyytle*, the April, Chaucerian bird-song of *lyyrrlr!* Observe the Rumanian *sbei*, the Germanic *stee to ho* (compare Siegfried, at the end of Act One singing to Tolstoy's disgust, *Heiho, Heiho! Aha! Oho! Aha! Heiaho!* You could easily add, *stee to ho!*). And then we come right into our own dialects with *yo go*, which, of course, is pure Birmingham.

The curious line at the end looks at first like the sort of thing that comes through on a teleprinter when they are testing it. But when we look carefully we see that 575757-

575 is an expression of ecstasy at the appearance of the word "lamb" which has suddenly come out right. We can appreciate the rational beauties of ordinary speech all the more after we have had these glimpses of the dark creative chaos from which it has emerged—the fascinating world of the gleece and the kank.

In this vast field which I have opened up there is great need for a proper, regularised, statistical method. There must be thousands of typewriter mediums like myself, and if our findings could be collated I am sure it would widen the whole field of modern psychology (there need be no conflict with existing science; you will notice the significant reference to *id* above). But the psychologists had better hurry up, while there still remain poople who xannot type.

FAR SPEAKING

There can be few words more seen and less read than the instructions in public telephone boxes. When we have pulled on three sides and at last found the one that opens, that is our last conscious, willed act; the rest is reflex. We stand on the little square of concrete, in our private world, our whole attention already on our correspondent; we are irritated by any delay, such as the maddeningly unhurried ratchety noise that goes on after we press Button B, as though very leisurely mice were hauling up tiny sacks with a block and tackle. We are certainly in no mood to read instructions.

Hardly anyone would admit to having actually learnt to telephone by reading the instructions from scratch. It

is true that, if we are townees, we do read in country
kiosks, to our surprise, that all we have to do is to lift the
receiver and listen for the operator; and we are mildly
interested in the thin little directory containing the
numbers of corn chandlers and farriers and the Regent
Kinema. But on the home ground our literary attention
is at its lowest level—a pity, because the instructions
contain the only attempt ever made by Post Office prose
writers, as far as I know, at romantic onomatopoeia—"a
high pitched burr-burr". It sounds like the scientific
definition of a West Country tenor.

This apathy has suddenly been disturbed, however, in a
number of London boxes, which have lately blossomed
out with instructions in French, German, Italian and
Spanish. They provide a fascinating comparative study,
and one's preconceptions about the languages are
curiously disturbed; in fact, it is only the Italian which
does what one would expect of it, when even a prosaic
thing like dialling tone is described as *un trillo basso
intermittente.*

The French is disappointing, for where one would
expect a kind of marble poetic style it is, in fact, technical
where it is not downright illogical. *Prière de s'adresser à
l'opératrice en anglais,* it begins. If they can address the
operator in English, why can't they read instructions in
English, hey? *Décrocher le recepteur a l'oreille et attendre le
son musical . . . introduire 2 pennies dans le dispositif d'encaissement.* There is admittedly a certain charm in the idea of
awaiting the musical sound, as though the box should
soon echo with a solemn passacaglia; but we are quickly
brought back to technology with the *dispositif d'encaissement,*
which sounds like the foundation of a suspension bridge.
The correspondent cannot hear you but after the man-

oeuvre of the button A, we are told with great formality; and *POUR RAPPELER L'OPERATRICE, agiter lentement le crochet commutateur*. Even the stolid English do not talk about the commutatory hook, preferring the fine conceit "cradle switch"; there is something illogical, too, about the injunction to agitate slowly; one thinks of a kind-hearted Communist who can't help liking his employer.

With the splendid German instructions, however, we step straight into the world of poetry and fairy-tales. The whole apparatus is treated animistically. *Sprechen sie bitte mit der Fernsprechbeamtin*, they begin, and somehow it couldn't matter less that here also one is invited to *sprechen* to her in English; for the marvellous word, *Fernsprechbeamtin*, has already evoked a vision of a placid, fair-haired, semi-mythical Teutonic figure, a kind of Telephone Queen, deep in some German forest—the Far-speaking Beaming One.

As in all fairy tales, there are mysterious commands and taboos to be observed: *dann zwei Pennies in den Automaten werfen*—then throw two Pennies in the Automaton. But *WENN SIE DIE GEWÜNSCHTE NUMMER NICHT KENNEN, kein Geld einwerfen:* if you do not know the Wished-for Number, do not throw in any Gold; if you do, the Automaton will probably clank ominously towards you in the thickening twilight, and you will hear behind you *ein schnarrender Laut*, the schnarring noise made by the dragon who also lives in the forest. But somehow Good will triumph. The *Fernsprechbeamtin* will appear at the crucial moment and wave her wand, and you will be joyously re-united with your Wished-for Number, and the *Fernsprechbeamtin* will let you choose three gifts from her palace.

I should choose E to K, L to R and S to Z to replace three of the four A to D's that are always in my box.

It is the peculiar genius of the French to express their philosophical thought in aphorisms, sayings hard and tight as diamonds, each one the crystal centre of a whole constellation of ideas. Thus, the entire scheme of seventeenth-century intellectual rationalism may be said to branch out from that single, pregnant saying of Descartes, *cogito ergo sum*—I think, therefore I am. Resistentialism, the philosophy which has swept present-day France, runs true to this aphoristic form. Go into any of the little cafés or *horlogeries* on Paris' Left Bank (make sure the Seine is flowing *away* from you, otherwise you'll be on the Right Bank, where *no* one is *ever* seen) and sooner or later you will hear someone say, "*Les choses sont contre nous.*"

"Things are against us." This is the nearest English translation I can find for the basic concept of Resistentialism, the grim but enthralling philosophy now identified with bespectacled, betrousered, two-eyed Pierre-Marie Ventre. In transferring the dynamic of philosophy from man to a world of hostile Things, Ventre has achieved a major revolution of thought, to which he himself gave the name "Resistentialism". Things (*res*) resist (*résister*) man (*homme*, understood). Ventre makes a complete break with traditional philosophic method. Except for his German precursors, Freidegg and Heidansiecker, all previous thinkers from the Eleatics to Marx have allowed at least some legitimacy to human thought and effort. Some, like Hegel or Berkeley, go so far as to make man's thought the supreme reality. In the Resistentialist cosmology, that is now the intellectual rage of Paris,

K*

Ventre offers us a grand vision of the Universe as One Thing—the Ultimate Thing (*Dernière Chose.*) And it is against us.

Two world wars have led to a general dissatisfaction with the traditional Western approach to cosmology, that of scientific domination. In Ventre's View, the World-Thing, to which he sometimes refers impartially as the Thing-World, opposes man's partial *stealing*, as it were, of consciousness—of his dividing it into the separate "minds" with which human history has made increasingly fatal attempts to create a separate world of men. Man's increase in this illusory domination over Things has been matched, *pari passu*, by the increasing hostility (and greater force) of the Things arrayed against him. Medieval man, for instance, had only a few actual Things to worry about—the lack of satisfactory illumination at night, the primitive hole in the roof blowing the smoke back and letting the rain in, and one or two other small Things like that. Modern, domesticated Western man has far more opportunities for battle-losing against Things—can-openers, collar-studs, chests of drawers, open man-holes, shoelaces. . . .

Now that Ventre has done it for us, it is easy to see that the reaction against nineteenth-century idealism begun by Martin Freidegg and Martin Heidansiecker was bound eventually to coalesce with the findings of modern physics in a philosophical synthesis for our time. Since much stress has been laid on the "scientific" basis of Resistential-ism, it will not be out of place here, before passing on to a more detailed outline of Ventre's thought, to give a brief account of those recent developments in physical science which have so blurred the line that separates it from metaphysics. It is an account which will surprise those whose acquaintance with Ventre is limited to reading reviews of his plays and who, therefore, are apt to think that Resistentialism is largely a matter of sitting inside a wet sack and moaning.

A convenient point of departure is provided by the famous Clark-Trimble experiments of 1935. Clark-Trimble was not primarily a physicist, and his great discovery of the Graduated Hostility of Things was made almost accidentally. During some research into the relation between periods of the day and human bad temper, Clark-Trimble, a leading Cambridge psychologist, came to the conclusion that low human dynamics in the early morning could not sufficiently explain the apparent hostility of Things at the breakfast table—the way honey gets between the fingers, the unfoldability of newspapers, etc. In the experiments which finally confirmed him in this view, and which he demonstrated before the Royal Society in London, Clark-Trimble arranged four hundred pieces of carpet in ascending degrees of quality, from coarse matting to priceless Chinese silk. Pieces of toast and marmalade, graded, weighed and measured, were then dropped on each piece of carpet, and the marmalade-downwards incidence was statistically analyzed. The toast fell right-side-up every time on the cheap carpet, except when the cheap carpet was screened from the rest (in which case the toast didn't know that Clark-Trimble had other and better carpets), and it fell marmalade-downwards every time on the Chinese silk. Most remarkable of all, the marmalade-downwards incidence for the intermediate grades was found to vary *exactly* with the quality of carpet.

The success of these experiments naturally switched Clark-Trimble's attention to further research on *resistentia*,

a fact which was directly responsible for the tragic and
sudden end to his career when he trod on a garden rake
at the Cambridge School of Agronomy. In the meantime,
Noys and Crangenbacker had been doing some notable
work in America. Noys carried out literally thousands of
experiments, in which subjects of all ages and sexes,
sitting in chairs of every conceivable kind, dropped
various kinds of pencils. In only three cases did the
pencil come to rest within easy reach. Crangenbacker's
work in the social-industrial field, on the relation of
human willpower to specific problems such as whether a
train or subway will stop with the door opposite you on a
crowded platform, or whether there will be a mail box
anywhere on your side of the street, was attracting much
attention.

Resistentialism, a sombre, post-atomic philosophy of
pagan, despairing nobility, advocates complete withdrawal from Things. Now that Ventre has done the
thinking for us it is easy to see how the soil was being
prepared for Resistentialism in the purely speculative
field by the thought of Martin Freidegg (1839–1904) and
Martin Heidansiecker (1850–1910), both well-known
anti-idealists and anti-intellectualists. It is in the latter's
Werke (Works) published at Tübingen in 1894, that the
word *Resistentialismus* first appears, although it has not the
definite meaning assigned to it by Ventre. It is now
possible to trace a clear line of development to Ventre
from Goethe, who said, with prophetic insight into the
hostility of one Thing, at least, "Three times has an apple
proved fatal. First to the human race, in the fall of Adam;
secondly to Troy, through the gift of Paris; and last of all,
to science through the fall of Newton's apple" (*Werke
XVI, 17*). Later we find Heidansiecker's concept of

Dingenhass, the hatred of Things. But in the confused terminology of this tortured German mystic we are never sure whether it is the Things who hate us, or we who hate the Things.

To the disillusioned youth of post-war France there was an immediate appeal in Ventre's relentlessly logical concept of man's destiny as a *néant*, or No-Thing, and it was the aesthetic expression of this that gave Resistentialism such great popular currency outside the philosophical textbooks, Ventre himself is an extra-ordinarily powerful dramatist; his first play, *Puits Clos*, concerns three old men who walk round ceaselessly at the bottom of a well. There are also some bricks in the well. These symbolise Things, and all the old men hate the bricks as much as they do each other. The play is full of their pitiful attempts to throw the bricks out of the top of the well, but they can, of course, never throw high enough, and the bricks always fall back on them. *Puits Clos* has only recently been taken off at the little Théatre Jambon to make room for another Resistentialist piece by Blanco del Huevo, called *Comment Sont Les Choses?* Del Huevo is an ardent young disciple of Ventre, and in this play, which is also running in London under the title *The Things That Are Caesar*, he makes a very bold step forward in the application of Resistentialist imagery to the theatre. He has made Things the characters, and reduced the human beings to what are known in Resistentialist language as *poussés*. The nearest English translation that suggests itself for this philosophical term is "pushed-arounds".

The chief "characters" in *Comment Sont Les Choses?* are thus a piano and a medicine cabinet; attached to the piano is *Poussé* Number One—no human beings are given actual names, because names are one of the devices by

which man has for so long blinded himself to his fundamental inability to mark himself out from the Universe
(*Dernière Chose*). *Poussé* Number One is determined to
play the piano, and the piano is determined to resist him.
For the first twenty minutes of Act I, he plays a Beethoven
sonata up to a certain bar, which always defeats him. He
stops, and plays this bar over a hundred times, very slowly.
He gets it right. He begins the sonata again and when he
gets to this bar he makes the very same mistake. He pours
petrol on the piano and is just about to set it on fire when
he hears a huge crash from the bathroom, also visible to
the audience on the other side of a stage partition.

All this time the medicine cabinet has been resisting

the attempts of *Poussé* Number Two to fix it on the wall, and it has now fallen into the bath. *Poussé* Number One who is in love, naturally, with *Poussé* Number Two's wife, *Pousée*, mimes his derision at the woeful lack of manhood of one who cannot even dominate Things to the extent of fixing a medicine cabinet. While he does so, the piano, with the tragic irony of a Greek chorus, speaks of *Poussé* Number One's own *hubris* and insolence in imagining that he can master the piano. *Poussé* Number Two is too busy to retaliate, as he is sweeping up the mess of camphorated oil, essence of peppermint, hair cream, calomine lotion, and broken glass towards the plug end of the bath, meaning to swill them out with hot water. He is desperately anxious to get this done before *Poussée* arrives home. She comes, however, while he is still trying ignominiously to get the bits of glass off one sticky hand with the other sticky hand, the glass then sticking to the other sticky hand and having to be got off with the first sticky hand (a good example of *choses co-rélatives* in the Resistentialist sense). *Poussée* expresses her scorn and asks her husband, all in mime, why he can't play the piano like *Poussé* Number One (who has persuaded her that he can). Eventually she goes out with *Poussé* Number One, and *Poussé* Number Two, exhausted by his labours at the bath, falls into it and into a deep coma.

Act II is extremely unconventional, and although some critics have hailed it as a great attempt to break down the modern separation between players and audience it seems to me to be the weakest part of the play, the nearest to a mere philosophical treatise. The curtain simply goes up on a Resistentialist exhibition, and the audience are invited to walk round. While they are examining the exhibits, which contain not only Resistentialist paintings but also what Ventre as well as Del Huevo calls *objects de vie* (chests of drawers, toothpaste caps, collar buttons, etc.), the stage manager comes on in his shirt sleeves and reads the chapter on sex from Ventre's *Résistentialisme*. Ventre takes a tragic view of sex, concerned as it is with the body, by which the World-Thing obtains its mastery over human territory. In so far as man is not merely a body he is only a pseudo-Thing (*pseudo-chose*), a logical "monster". Ventre sees woman, with her capacity for reproduction

indefinitely prolonging this state of affairs, as the chief cause of humanity's present dilemma of Thing-separation and therefore Thing-warfare. Love between humans, i.e. between Man (Not-woman) and Woman (Not-man), perpetuates bodies as Things, because a man, in being a Not-woman, shows the capacity of all things for being only *one* Thing (it is all much clearer in the French, of course). Just as a man is a Not-woman, he is also a Not-sideboard, a Not-airplane. But this is as far as man can go in Thing-ness, and if it were not for women we could all die and be merged comfortably in the Universe or Ultimate Thing.

In Act III, the action, if one can call it that, is resumed. When the curtain goes up *Poussé* Number Two is discovered still lying in the bath. The tragedy of man's futile struggle against the power of Things begins to draw towards its fatal climax as we hear a conversation between the piano and the medicine cabinet in which the piano suggests an exchange of their respective *Poussés*. The piano, realising that *Poussée* doesn't know anything about music anyway and will probably accept *Poussé* Number One's word that he can play, queering the pitch for Things, with this ambivalent concept of love, wishes to lure Number Two on instead. (In Ventre's system, Things are quite capable of emanations and influences by reason of their affinity with man's Thing-body or Not-other). Accordingly, when *Poussé* Number Two wakes up in the bath he feels a compulsive desire to play the piano, forgetting that his fingers are still sticky—and of course it is not his piano anyway. The piano, biding its time, lets him play quite well. (In Resistentialist jargon, which unashamedly borrows from the terminology of Gonk and others when necessary, the resistance of the I-Thing is infinite and that of the Thou-Thing is zero—it is always *my* bootlaces that break—and of course *Poussé* Number Two thinks he is playing *Poussé* Number One's piano). Number Two only leaves the instrument when he hears the others coming back. He goes to the bathroom and listens through the partition with a knowing smile as *Poussé* Number One begins to play for *Poussée*. Naturally, *his* fingers stick to the keys the piano being an I-Thing for him, or so he thinks. This makes *Poussé* Number Two feel so good that he actually manages to fix the medicine cabinet. *Poussée*, returning to him disillusioned from the pseudo-pianist, flings herself into his arms, but it is too late. He has cut an artery on a piece of the broken glass sticking out of the medicine cabinet. In despair she rushes back to the music room, where *Poussé* Number One has just lit a cigarette to console himself and think out the next move. ("As if that mattered," says the piano scornfully.) As she comes in there is a great explosion. *Poussé* Number One has forgotten the petrol he had poured on the piano in Act I.

The drama is not the only art to have been revivified in France (and therefore everywhere) by Resistentialism. This remorseless modern philosophy has been reflected in the work of all the important younger composers and painters in Paris. Resistentialist music, based on acceptance of the tragic Thing-ness, and therefore limitation, of musical instruments, makes use of a new scale based on the Absolute Mathematical Reluctance of each instrument. The A.M.R. of the violin, for instance, is the critical speed beyond which it is impossible to play it because of the strings' melting. The new scale is conceived, says Dufay, as "a geometric rather than a tonic progression. Each note is seen as a point on the circumference of a circle of which the centre is the A.M.R. The circle must then be conceived as *inside-out*". Dufay has expressed in mathematical terms that cosmic dissatisfaction of the artist with the physical medium in which he is forced to work. Kodak, approaching the problem from a different angle, has taken more positive steps to limit the "cosmic offence-power" of the conventional scale by *reducing* the number of notes available. His first concerto, for solo tympanum and thirty conductors, is an extension of the argument put forward some years ago, in remarkable anticipation of Resistentialism, by Ernest Newman, music critic of the London *Sunday Times*, who said that the highest musical pleasure was to be derived much more from score-reading than from actual performance. Kodak is now believed to be working on a piece for conductors only.

I have left Resistentialism in painting to the end because it is over the quarrel between Ventre and Afga, at one time his chief adherent among the artists, that the little cafés and bistos of the Quartier Latin are seething to-day. When Agfa first came under Ventre's influence he accepted the latter's detachment, not so much Franciscan as Olympic, from Things. His method was to sit for hours in front of a canvas brooding over disasters, particularly earthquakes, in which Things are hostile in the biggest and most obvious way. Sometimes he would discover that the canvas had been covered during his abstraction, sometimes not. At any rate, Agfa enjoyed a *succès fou* as a painter of earthquakes and recently he has shown himself impatient of the thoroughgoing *néantisme* (no-thingery) of Ventre, who insists relentlessly that to conform completely to the pure Resistentialist ideal a picture should not only have no paint but should be without canvas and without frame, since, as he irrefutably points out, these Things are all Things (*ces choses sont toutes des choses.*)

The defection of Agfa and of other "moderates" among the Resistentialists has been brought to a head by the formation, under a thinker named Qwertyuiop, of a neo-Resistentialist group. The enthusiasm with which medieval students brawled in the streets of Paris over the Categories of Being has lost none of its keenness to-day, and the recent pitched battle between Ventristes and

followers of Qwertyuiop outside the Café aux Fines
Herbes, by now famous as Ventre's headquarters, has, if
nothing else, demonstrated that Paris still maintains her
position as the world's intellectual centre. It is rather
difficult to state the terms of the problem without using
some of the Resistentialists' phraseology, so I hope I may
be pardoned for briefly introducing it.

Briefly, the issue is between Ventre, the pessimist, and
Qwertyuiop, the optimist. Ventre, in elaborating on his
central aphorism, *les choses sont contre nous*, distinguishes
carefully between what he calls *chose-en-soi*, the Thing in
itself, and *chose-pour-soi*, the Thing *for* itself. *Chose-en-soi* is
his phrase for Things existing in their own right, sublimely
and tragically independent of man. In so far as Ventre's
pregnant terminology can be related to traditional
western categories, *chose-en-soi* stands for the Aristotelean
outlook, which tends to ascribe a certain measure of
reality to Things without reference to any objective Form
in any mind, human or divine. There are even closer
parallels with the later, medieval philosophy of Nominal-
ism, which says, roughly, that there are as many Things
as we can find names for; Ventre has an interesting passage
about what he calls inversion (*inversion*) in which he
exploits to the full the contrast between the multiplicity
of actions which Things can perform against us—from a
slightly overhanging tray falling off a table when the
removal of one lump of sugar over-balances it, to the
atomic bomb—and the paucity of our vocabulary of
names on such occasions.

The third great concept of Ventre is *le néant* (the No-
Thing). Man is ultimately, as I have said, a No-Thing, a
metaphysical monster doomed to battle, with increasing
non-success, against real Things. Resistentialism, with

what Ventre's followers admire as stark, pagan courage, bids man abandon his hopeless struggle.

Into the dignified tragic, Olympian detachment of Ventre's "primitive" Resistentialism the swarthy, flamboyant Qwertyuiop has made a startling, meteoric irruption. Denounced scornfully by the Ventristes as a plagiarist. Qwertyuiop was, indeed, at one time a pupil of Ventre. He also asserts the hostility of Things to man— but he sees grounds for hope in the concept of *chose-pour-soi* (the Thing for itself) with which it is at least possible to enter into relationship. But he is more a dramatist than a philosopher, and what enrages the Ventristes is the bouncing optimism of his plays and also the curious symbolic figure of the *géant* or giant which appears in them all. This *géant* is a kind of Resistentialist version of Nietzsche's superman, a buskined, moustachioed figure who intervenes, often with great comic effect, just when the characters in the play are about to jump down a well (the well is, of course, a frequent Resistentialist symbol— cf. Ventre's own *Puits Clos*).

The Ventristes point out acidly that in the first edition of *Résistentialisme* the word *géant* appears throughout as a misprint for *néant*. Friction between the two groups was brought to a head by Qwertyuiop's new play *Messieurs, Les Choses Sont Terribles*, (loosely, *Gentlemen, Things are Terrible*). On the first night at the Théâtre des Somnambules, the Ventristes in the gallery created an uproar and had to be expelled when, at the end of the second act, the inevitable *géant* had stepped in to prevent three torturings, seven betrayals, and two suicides. The battle was renewed later with brickbats and bottles when Qwertyuiop and his followers interrupted one of Ventre's *choseries*, or Thing-talks, at the Café aux Fines Herbes.

Five of the moderates and two Ventristes were arrested by the gendarmerie and later released on bail. All Paris is speculating on the outcome of the trial, at which many important literary figures are expected to give evidence.

It is, however, not in the law courts that the influence of Resistentialism on our time will be decided. It is in the little *charcuteries* and *épiceries* of the Left Bank. It is in the stimulating mental climate of Paris that the artists and dramatists will decide for themselves whether there is any future for art in the refined philosophical atmosphere to which Ventre's remorseless logic would have them penetrate. Although Qwertyuiop has succeeded in attracting many of Ventre's more lukewarm followers among the arts, who had begun to rebel against the Master's uncompromising insistence on pictures without paint and music without instruments, without any Things at all, there seems no doubt that Ventre is the greater thinker, and it is an open question whether he will achieve his object of persuading the world to abandon Things without the indispensable help of the artistic confraternity in moulding public opinion.

There is no doubt, either, that Ventre's thought strikes a deep chord in everyone during these sombre, post-atomic times. Ventre has, I think, liberated the vast flood of creative hatred which makes modern civilization possible. My body, says Ventre, is *chose-en-soi* for me, a Thing which I cannot control, a Thing which uses me. But it is *chose-pour-soi* for the Other. I am thus a Hostile Thing to the Other, and so is he to me. At the same time it follows (or it does in the French) that I am a No-Thing to the world. But I cannot be united or merged with the World-Thing because my Thing-Body, or Not-other gives me an illicit and tragically deceptive claim on existence and "happiness". I am thus tragically committed to extending the area of my always illusory control over the Thing-body—and as the "mind" associated with my Thing-body is merely the storing up of recollected struggles with Things, it follows that I cannot know the Other except as one of the weapons with which the World-Thing has increased its area of hostile action.

Resistentialism thus formalizes hatred both in the cosmological and in the psychological sphere. It is becoming generally realized that the complex apparatus of our modern life—the hurried meals, the dashing for trains, the constant meeting of people who are seen only as "functions"—the barman, the wife, etc.—could not operate if our behaviour were truly dictated by the old, reactionary categories of human love and reason. This is where Ventre's true greatness lies. He has transformed, indeed reversed the traditional mechanism of thought, steered it away from the old dogmatic assumption that we could use Things, and cleared the decks for the evolution of the Thing-process without futile human opposition. Ventre's work brings us a great deal nearer to the realization of the Resistentialist goal summed up in the words, "Every Thing out of Control."

SIT STILL, THERE.

There is really only one class of people
Whom I'd like to push off a very high steeple,
Whom I'd wish to get caught in textile machinery
Or baked to death in a Heinz baked beanery;
All sendable plagues I would willingly send
ON PEOPLE WHO LEAVE BEFORE THE END.
They creak up aisles in the midst of finales,
After coat-strugglings, bag-clickings, whispered parleys,
They kick your gloves as they scramble past
Just when the heroine breathes her last.
Are their horrible homes so far away
That the 9.28's the last train to-day?
Are they rushing away to a sale at Grantham
Or can't they abide the National Anthem?
Where are they going, with self-importance
That scorns politeness's Oughts and Oughtn'ts?

But why go on? For I cannot expect
This fine moral poem to have an effect
Since none of the people for whom it is penned
Will be decent enough to read to
        THE END.